IMPLICATIONS OF JUDICIAL ACTIVISM ON INDIAN JUDICIARY

AN ANALYSIS

IMPLICATIONS OF JUDICIAL ACTIVISM ON INDIAN JUDICIARY

AN ANALYSIS

Dr. GOVIND KUMAR SAXENA

ZORBA BOOKS

ZORBA BOOKS

Published by Zorba Books, February 2022

Website: www.zorbabooks.com
Email: info@zorbabooks.com

Title :- **IMPLICATIONS OF JUDICIAL ACTIVISM ON INDIAN JUDICIARY-AN ANALYSIS**

Printbook ISBN :- 978-93-93029-77-5

Zorba Books Pvt. Ltd. (opc)
Sushant Arcade,
Next to Courtyard Marriot,
Sushant Lok 1, Gurgaon – 122009, India

Printed by Thomson Press (India) Ltd.

B-315, Okhla Industrial Area, Phase 1, New Delhi- 110020

CONTENTS

ACKNOWLEDGEMENT

Completing this book, I stand here today reflecting on all those who have made this effort a pleasant and memorable experience.

It gives me immense pleasure to express my profound gratitude to each individual who helped me complete this book in its present form. If this small effort has seen the light of the day, it is undoubtedly due to the good wishes of the ever-inspiring, supportive souls who have evinced keen interest in my work, by virtue of their eminence.

I am immensely thankful to **Major General Praveen Kumar Sharma (Retd.),** Director, Amity Law School, Amity University Gurugram, Haryana for his kind support and guidance through every juncture of this work. He always took utmost interest with constant encouragement, to ensure timely completion of my work. Without their tremendous and valuable support, co-operation, and continuous encouragement this work which had been submitted as a thesis for my Ph.D. would not have been a success.

I take this opportunity to express how deeply indebted I am to **Professor Dr. Ajay Kumar Bhatt,** Amity Law School Amity University Haryana.

I am greatly thankful to **Mr. Pranshul Pathak**, Coordinator & Associate Professor, Amity Law School, Amity University Haryana, for his constant help and support.

I am sincerely thankful to **Professor Dr. Hemant Sharma**, of Amity Business School for his valuable help and guidance. I am truly thankful to **Dr. Bhavna Singh** for her most humble help and support.

I am extremely thankful to **Mr. Himanshu Shekhar**, Advocate, High Court Allahabad, a very learned man, for his never-ending, sincere co-operation.

I would like to mention my most special thanks and heartfelt gratitude to my father **Shri Hari Om Saxena**, my brothers **Shri Pankaj Kumar Saxena, Dr. Dhiraj Kumar Saxena,** and my wife **Archana** for giving me all the moral support at every stage, throughout the progress and completion of this work. I would also like to specially mention my immensely helpful son **Tejas** and lovely Daughter **Tavisha**.

Last but not the least; I thank **God** for his blessings and making it all possible.

My special thanks and gratitude to Zorba Books for publishing this book within a short period with high quality. I hope that the book would be very useful to all the stakeholders of the legal field in the country. Suggestions are welcomed.

DR. GOVIND KUMAR SAXENA

PLACE: PRAYAGRAJ

DATE:19, February 2022

"A Constitution states or ought to state not law for the passing hour, but principles for an expanding future."

Benjamin N. Cardozo

PRELUDE

Delivery of justice has always been a challenging task and will remain so for as long as mankind exists. With a large population, the task becomes more challenging. Over one billion people live in India, a country rich in cultures, languages, and religions.

A single wrong step is enough to set the whole country adrift. In this regard, the overlapping powers of nations' administrators cause few concerns.

India established democracy after the British model of Parliamentary government. In addition to representing the people, it represented their will.

Each government consists of three pillars of function whose aid is required to represent the people's will.

Legislators make laws; the Executive makes sure laws are enforced; and the Judiciary decides how the law should be applied to cases where the law is broken. However, even when acting within the scope of their powers, there is often overlapping of functions between them.[1]

The principle of 'Separation of powers' is noticeable in the works of Locke and Aristotle[2], however, the French philosopher, Montesquieu[3], is owed for its roots. When acknowledged in their true form, the principle specified that every organ of the Constitution must be operate within its domain, with no overlap in their functioning. Furthermore, it does try in bringing exclusivity in the operation, as well as the powers with precise demarcation. This principle also concretes that a government must not let all three powers to be implemented by an individual (or a group).

Further, it is necessary for the power-bearers to be balanced for a stable political system. The minds behind the Indian Constitution

1 M. J. C. Vile, Constitutionalism and Separation of Powers (Liberty Fund Inc., Indianapolis, 2nd ed., 1967).

2 C.K.Thakker, Administrative Law 31 (Eastern Book Company, 1992).

3 Charles de Secondat, Baron de Montesquieu, The Spirit of Law (French: De l'esprit des lois) (1748).

never had the intention of adopting such a principle in its complete form. Thus, the American 'limited government' doctrine was preferred over the British Parliamentary sovereignty.[4]

James Madison explained Montesquieu as –

"The accumulation of all powers, legislative, executive and judicial, in the same hands whether of one, a few, or many and whether hereditary, self-appointed or elective, may justly be pronounced as the very definition of tyranny."[5]

Dr. B. R. Ambedkar clearly stated his views before the Constituent Assembly in his speech about laying down a system of checks over the authority of the Government's three organs. He said:

"The purpose of a Constitution is not merely to create the organs of the State but to limit their authority, because, if no limitation is imposed upon the authority of the organs, there will be complete tyranny and complete oppression… It would result in utter chaos."[6]

Analysis of several Constitutional provisions makes it clear that, at least in theory, the functions of various organs have been differentiated. This has been done to ensure that no organ encroaches upon the functions of another organ. However, it is not easy to accurately observe the separation of powers doctrine if detaching the "checks and balances", as provided. Wade expresses that Montesquieu was critical about the monopoly as well as accumulation instead of interactions. Therefore, mutual restraint in the exercise of their respective powers is the soul of the doctrine. In India, these checks and balances are seen to be spread out in the Constitution and laws limiting the powers granted to the respective bearers to prevent *'The Tyranny'* as projected by Dr. Ambedkar.

Thereby, among the three organs, none of them can appropriate for any other organ, any essential function, not even through a

4 D. D. Basu, Introduction to the Constitution of India (LexisNexis Butterworths Wadhwa, 20th Edition, Reprint 2011).

5 The Federalist No. 48, at 276 (James Madison) (Clinton Rossiter ed., 1999).

6 C.A.D (Vol. IX) 1659-63.

constitution amendment. And, even if these amendments are made; they will be struck down, considering them to be unconstitutional.[7]

In India's version of constitutional democracy, the most sacred role is played by judicial institutions. Any person, who perceives any of his fundamental rights to be violated, can approach to Supreme Court under to the Article 32. By Article 13(2), Supreme Court can declare a law as null and void, if it violates any of the fundamental right guaranteed under the Constitution. A much wider jurisdiction is endowed in the High Courts, for entertaining various other kinds of petitions. Be it for fundamental rights, enforcement, or any other grounds. The Supreme Court is vested with power for deciding if State Legislature/Parliament has passed a law that goes past its assigned domain.

Further, the Supreme Court is vested with the power to pass such order/decree as it finds imperative, in any case, or matter presented before it, to meet the ends for delivering justice. Such provisions incorporate the court's inherent powers of discretion, without any restriction related to the circumstance/cases that could necessitate the exercise of its power. It is devoid of any condition which may be needed to be fulfilled before the exercise of these powers. The court itself, however, across several judgments has stated that, there should not be any misuse of Article 142, for building a new turf that didn't exist before. It should not attempt to indirectly accomplish something, which could not be achieved directly.[8]

This doctrine is supremely intricate, with *accrescent* subjects. Its applicable scope and extent vary with every case. Ever since our constitution came into existence, the legitimacy of the power of courts concerning the legislature has often been questioned. An evaluation of how the constitution makers integrated provisions related to the judiciary indicates that they were supremely inclined to ensuring

7 C. K. Takwani, Lectures on Administrative Law 33-37 (Eastern Book Company, Lucknow, 2004).

8 Delhi Judicial Service Assocn. v. State of Gujarat AIR 1991 SC 2176; Union Carbide Corpn v. U.O.I. AIR 1992 SC 248; Supreme Court Bar Association v. U.O.I. AIR 1998 SC 1895; State of Punjab v. Rajesh Syal AIR 2002 SC 3687 etc.

the judiciary's independence. All their attempts were aimed towards enabling and ensuring the judiciary's ability to effectively discharge its judicial review's wide powers, for protecting the people of India and their rights.[9]

Except for their conventional role of resolving disputes among interest of the parties, there is a need for the judicial institutions to provide a balanced system for the divergent pressures and proves to be a watchkeeper for the society. The crux behind the principle of separation of powers is to establish polarity, for avoiding chance of displaying authoritarianism by government's any one organ. Therefore, the principle has been embraced with its balances and checks, in the absence of which, no constitutional democracy can survive in today's world.[10]

Another relevant aspect is that the courts of law are themselves acting as creators and modifiers of the Constitution while also being critically instrumental for achieving the country's ideals preserved within. The makers of the Indian Constitution took great care to ensure an impartial and independent judiciary as Constitution's interpreter. To act as a guardian of citizen's rights, it was endowed with power of 'Judicial Review'.[11]

Broadly speaking, there exist three aspects of Judicial Review – Legislative, Administrative and Judicial. However, the judiciary cannot exercise this power without considering the wisdom behind the legislative policies.[12] It must be extra cautious since this has the power to hold any law unconstitutional and thus unenforceable.

The Courts are often, under the guise of interpreting the law, go a step ahead, and end up with new interpretations and precedents that

9 Granville Austin, The Indian Constitution: Cornerstone of a Nation 173-175 (Oxford University Press, 1972)."

10 Indira Gandhi v. Rajnarain AIR 1975 SC 2299; State of Bihar v. Balmukund Shah AIR 2000 SC 1296; Ram Jawaya v. State of Punjab AIR 1955 SC 549.

11 Constitution of India, Art. 13

12 M. P. Jain, Indian Constitutional Law (Wadhwa & Company, Nagpur, 5th edition, 2008). 22 Henry J. Abraham, The Judicial Process 296 (Oxford University Press, 1980)

are applicable throughout the country. Such laws are commonly not the same as that of pre-existing ones. This act is known as "Judicial Activism". In a modern society, which is experiencing constant social and economic changes, the age-old traditional interpretation of the constitution would invariably lose its relevance. Judicial activism thus seems to be inseparable from judicial review.[13] The Court makes a liberal interpretation of the constitutional provisions. They are obligated by the very distribution of powers to keep the constitution up to date with changing modern times. A Court that utilizes a dynamic interpretation and gives an altogether new meaning to any provision of law is called an 'activist court'. It does so for suiting the modifying economic and social conditions, or for expanding the horizon of an individual's rights.

Protecting the rule of law as well as upholding the constitution is the Judiciary's primary duty.[14] Its responsibility of being the faithful protector of the constitution is of crucial importance in any democracy. The legal system is kept vibrant by an independent and impartial judiciary. Furthermore, the Indian judiciary is described as a creative one. The credibility of the judicial process is eventually based on the manner of the justice administered.

Judicial functions can be explained as:

- *a balancing wheel of the federation;*
- *which keep equilibrium among fundamental rights and social justice;*
- *which keep all forms of authorities within the bounds; and*
- *which control the Administrative Tribunals*

The judiciary have been vested with powers of being the final arbiter of constitutional disputes under various democratic Constitutions. Indian Constitution, greatly influenced by the Constitution of the United States of America is no different.

---

13 Ibid.

14 Justice K.G. Balakrishnan (Former Chief Justice), Interview in India Today, Jan. 22, 2007.

The Indian Constitution derives its guidance from the preamble, *Justice – political, economic, and social.* Furthermore, one of the primary concepts is social justice which is the essence of Part III and IV of the constitution, concerning the economic development and social justice of the citizens. Also, the judiciary must promote social justice through its judgments. However, during adjudication when judicial discretion is applied, the judiciary must be very careful. It should primarily promote social justice and in situations where it deems necessary, interpret the law to introduce new rules, thereby excluding the policies introduced by other organs.

Quoting Justice Cardozo's expression about a Judge's role of interpretation:

"He (judge) legislates only between gaps. He fills the open spaces in the law".[15]

Justice A.M. Ahmadi, former CJI said:

"Judicial Activism is a necessary adjunct of the judicial function ever since the protection of public interest, as opposed to private interest, happens to be its main concern".[16]

While Cardozo emphasized upon the role of subjective elements in the nature of the judicial function, which distinguishes between whether the judge making the law or declaring the law, in the present day, it is universally acknowledged that the Judge inevitably acts as the '*lawmaker*' when the judiciary is entrusted with the important function of legislation's judicial review as well as an administrative action.[17]

The Supreme Court in one of the early and landmark "*Bandhua Mukti Morcha* case"[18] observed that:

"There is great merit in the court proceedings to decide an issue based on strict legal principle & avoiding the influence of an emotional appeal. For that alone, gives the decision of the court a direction that is certain

15 Cardozo, supra note 1 at 113.

16 A. M. Ahmadi, Judicial Process: Social Legitimacy and Institutional Viability, 4 SCC (Jour) 1-10 (1996)."

17 Cardozo, supra note 1.

18 Bandhua Mukti Morcha v. Union of India 1984 1 SCC 161, 234."

and unfaltering, and that extraordinary permanence in legal jurisprudence makes it a base for a step forward in the progress of law. Indeed, both certainties of substance and direction are indispensable in the development of the law and are to be invested with credibility to command public confidence in its legitimacy."[19]

The Court should always take care, not to overstep its limits of the judicial function. It should avoid trespassing into the areas that constitution has reserved for the legislature & executive. Apex judiciary cannot interfere with any statutory or constitutional provisions that is prescribed as clear violation. However, if there has been a considered policy decision, not in dispute or not intentional, then the court won't review the appropriate area, which is domain of the executive. It will not be in the public interest.[20]

When two or more views or options are feasible and after their due consideration, a policy decision has been taken by the government, it is not the court's function to investigate the matter by itself or sit in appeal over such policy decisions like *Balco v. Union of India.*[21] Whatsoever technique is implemented in adjudication by the judiciary, the procedure must be in coherence with the judicial principles.

Any democratic nation wants a non-political, incorruptible, independent, and fearless judiciary practicing with wisdom its formidable power of judicial review. Every republic's heart is an independent judiciary. The democracy's basis, the root of its perennial vitality, is the requirement for its development as well as the promise of its good.[22] The law is not static; it is evolving with the ever-evolving culture. It must be changed considering the transitions that comes with time. For the very reasons to accommodate this, the Indian Supreme Court finds its purpose to exercise judicial review.

---

19 Ibid.

20 S. P. Sathe, Judicial Activism iIn India: Transgressing Boarders and Enforcing Limits 308 (Oxford University Press, 2nd ed, 2002)."

21 Balco v. Union of India (2002) 2 SCC 333.

22 H.R Khanna, Independence of the Judiciary, 16(3) SCC J. (1981).

Justice Kuldip Singh, & Justice S. Ratnavel Pandian, in "*S.P. Gupta v. Union of India*"[23], observed:

"The proposition that the provisions of the Constitution must be confined not only to the interpretation which the framers, with the conditions & outlook of their time would have placed upon them, will not be tenable and is liable to be dropped for more than one reasoning - firstly, some of the current issues couldn't have been foreseen; secondly, other would not have been discussed and thirdly, yet some may have been leftover as controversial issues, i.e. termed as deferred issues with conflicting intentions. Beyond these reasons, it is not easy or possible to decipher as to what were the factors which influenced the minds of the framers at the time of framing the Constitution when it is juxtaposed to the present time. The inevitable truth is that law is not static & immutable but ever-increasingly dynamic and grows with the ongoing passage of time. It is not enough merely interpreting the Constitutional text. It must be interpreted to advance the policy & purpose underlying its provisions."

It was further observed,

"A purposeful meaning, which may have come necessarily by the passage of time and process of experience, has to be given. The Courts should face the fact and meet the needs & aspirations of the times. The Constitution has not only to be read in the light of contemporary circumstances and values; it has to be read in such a way that the circumstances and values of present generation are given expression in its provisions".[24]

'Amendment of Constitution' - a provision contained in Part- XX Article 368(1) is one of its well-known features.

The particular provision resulted to be extremely controversial matter and led to disagreement among the judiciary and parliament as evidenced in *Shankari Prasad*[25], *Golaknath*[26], and *Keshavananda Bharti*[27].

23 S.P.Gupta v. Union of India (1981) Supp SCC 87.
24 Ibid.
25 Shankari Prasad v. Union of India AIR 1951 SC 458.
26 I.C Golaknath v. State of Punjab AIR 1967 SC 1643.
27 Keshavanand Bharti v. State of Kerala AIR 1973 SC 1461.

Judges scarcely took cognizance of the challenge to the validity of the legislative actions, except when they appear to be ultra-virus. However, they vigilantly investigated the conduct of the executive where they violated their authority and found them to be unconstitutional. The fundamental idea is that courts must interpret the constitution based on the existing stipulations, rather than reading it based on what it 'ought to be'. With the persuasion of the government for the development of a Bill of Rights in Indian Constitution by passing the Government of India Act, 1935, the country gradually started experiencing a transition from the conventional judicial position towards a more participatory one.

1. BACKGROUND

An imperative concept accepted concerning the higher legal executive, particularly the Supreme Court, is its alleged extremist approach. The word 'legal activism' has no single definition. It implies various things to various individuals. It could mean dynamism to judges, legal inventiveness to a few, legal enactment to others, and a push towards bringing 'social unrest' through the legal executive to some others.

To understand the idea of legal activism the j

ob allotted under the constitution must be comprehended appropriately. The Indian Constitution explicitly lays down that all three organs of the State must independently perform their respective functions, with no encroachment on the functions of the other two. However, according to the society's interest as well as to harmonize the prevailing inconsistencies, Judges must have the permission to go for reasonable ethical, moral, and rational considerations as and when needed.

In India, there exists a truly 'one of a kind' situation for legal activism. The arrangement for the cure of an issue or welfare of an individual is existing, yet the sufferer considering his numbness and neediness considers himself unfit to look for legal redressal or thump the entryway of the Courts. Comprehending this scenario, the higher court adopted certain changes and relaxations with equity for the benefit of such a dismissed, poor, and uninformed man. To deliver equal justice to the huge and overflowing population of this nation, the triumvirate of Judges during the eighties of the twentieth century allowed agent appeal, loosening up the standard of locus standi. They began treating letters and news reports as writ requests, by taking *suo motu* cognizance of the matters concerning provocation, misuse, brutality, medical laxity, police barbarity, separation, and assertion by the officers, etc.

Without the exact and exquisite meaning of the expression 'legal activism', it is important to rethink the elements of the legal executive.

To assess the job of the legal executive in a vote-based system like India, an outline of the lobbyist role pretended by the legal executive must be ascertained.

Seeds of legal activism should be followed through the *Boner's* case wherein Lord Coke of England propounded the principle for a decree to stay away from an act of Parliament when it is against the privilege and reasons, repulsive or difficult to be performed. From that point onwards, various cases in England were adjudicated accordingly and an entire range of Law of Torts was developed.

The history of legal activism in the United States of America begins from *Marbury v. Madison* wherein Chief Justice John Marshal refuted the enactment authorized by the American Congress and advanced the Doctrine of Judicial Review of Acts that was subsequently passed by the American Congress.

History of the 'Judicial Activism' in India since 1950 shows a walk from 'Authoritative Superiority' to 'Legal Supremacy'. By assuming an extremist job, the higher judiciary has been occupied with advancing and ensuring the protection of the objectives reflected in the preamble of the constitution.

The high-water instance of legal activism in India was *Keshavananda Bharti v. State of Kerala*[28] where a precept of the basic structure has been proposed by the Supreme Court. From that point onwards, the Apex Court now and again has been embracing the dissident job. In this line, notable cases are *Maneka Gandhi v. Union of India29*; *Advocates on Record Association v. Union of India*[30](wherein over judicial transfers and appointments, the authority of Chief Justice of India was recognized and backed by the majority verdict); *Manohar Joshi v. Nitin Bhaurao Patil & Anr*[31], *I.R. Coelho v. State of Tamil Nadu*[32] (also known as 9th Schedule Case) (this unanimous judgment delivered by a 9-judges bench led by Chief Justice Sabharwal, upheld the validity of

28 Supra at 28.
29 AIR 1978 SC 597.
30 AIR 1994 SC 268.
31 1996 AIR 796.
32 2007 (2) SCC 1: 2007 AIR(SC) 861."

the 'Principle of Basic Structure' propounded in *Keshavananda Bharti*. The Court again upheld the power of the Judiciary to review any such law which in its opinion could in any way, destroy the basic structure of the Constitution.

In India, Judicial activism dates to the constitution's very commencement. India was declared as the Sovereign, Democratic, Republic, aiming to create a "Welfare State" protecting justice for its people – political, economic, and social.

India's first Prime Minister, Pt. Jawaharlal Nehru strongly believed that no Court (not even the Supreme Court), could contest these guidelines, as he was so determined for implementing the welfare scheme. This is obvious from his loud, furious, and confrontational speech on 9 August 1947 in the Constituent Assembly. Furthermore, it can be observed through his anger shown in the debates of Constituent Assembly:

"No Supreme Court and no judiciary can stand in judgment over the sovereign will of the Parliament that represents the will of an entire community. If we go wrong here and there, it can point it out but in the ultimate analysis, where the future of the community is concerned, no judiciary can come in the way."[33]

Parliamentary supremacy influences even the courts. It has been believed by the courts that law is considered as what Parliament has declared as well as it was their duty of interpreting the laws as it is, as well as upholding them. Thus, during the pre-emergency Nehruvian era, it can be noted that, in India, judicial activism was predisposed to the ideals of the great personality Pt. Jawaharlal Nehru.

M.P. Jain, in his book, 'Indian Constitutional Law'[34], mentions that the Indian judicial approach was positivist during the Nehruvian period. Through implementing the similar stringent interpretation canons as applicable to common laws, the court simply read the Constitutional document. Furthermore, in *Chiranjit Lal Chowdhuri v.*

33 Rajeev Dhavan, Nehru, Law and Social Change, 45-62, Rajeev Dhavan & Thomas Paul, (eds.), Nehru and The Constitution (Indian Law Institute, New Delhi 1992).

34 Supra note 13

Union of India[35], Mukherjee J. has jurisdictionally set the principle, in which it has been observed by the Court:

"In interpreting the provisions of our Constitution, we should go by the plain words used by the Constitution makers."

For interpretation of the Constitution, Article 367 (1) has been looked at by the courts. The Courts failed to see through the terms laid out in the Constitution or use the constitutional spirit as an aid for reading the Constitution by following the principle of literal interpretation. Article 367 (1) postulates:

"Unless the context otherwise requires, the General Clauses Act, 1897, shall, subject to any adaptations, modifications that may be made therein under Article 372 apply for the interpretation of this Constitution as it applies for the interpretation of an Act of the Legislature of the Dominion of India."

Durga Das Basu, a prominent jurist has supported the exercise of literal interpretation of Indian Constitution, observing that Article 367(1) itself embodies the principle of statutory construction, however, he varies on the point that the judicial response to the Constitution has been no more and exclusively a statutory interpretation alone.

The Court tried to promote the ideals of federalism during the Nehruvian period. Even their decisions were mainly centrist. Although certain rulings were also taken in favour of the regional States, the Court had made a rather liberal view of the Centre's control. But in the post-Nehruvian era, the executive & the parliament were warring together on one hand, with the judiciary on the other. In Parliament, the Executive has reaffirmed its authority to regulate the fundamental rights and change the constitution in any respect. The Supreme Court, on the other hand, affirmed its authority over constitutional reforms. It culminated in the legal invention of the 'prospective overruling' doctrine and the 'basic structure' doctrine. The Supreme Court's gradual transformation from a positivist court to an activist court is judicial activism's another aspect.

35 1951 AIR 41, 1950 SCR 869

John Gardner[36] agreed that the judge-made law was constitutionally legitimate when it was declared, followed, invoked, enacted by certain judges, approved by some, or otherwise were involved at the relevant time and place. Justice P. N. Bhagwati, former Indian Chief Justice, advocated the validity of those judges' legislative positions. The learned judge claimed that regulation is an intrinsic and necessary aspect of the judicial process and that judges shouldn't feel timid or excused for this role in the development of laws.

Furthermore, the book 'Introduction to the Constitution of India' authored by Durga Das Basu, has been critical about judicial innovations because bitterness between the Judiciary with the Legislature can be engendered through it, in case where one of them tries checkmating the other, through judicial activism or amendment.

During the pre-emergency era, there was a transformation of the Supreme Court from a literal interpreter to a liberal interpreter and back to being a literal interpreter during the emergency era. However, the Supreme Court of India again took legal advocacy in a desirable political way to eliminate its derogatory reputation created during the emergency period.

The Court has again played a lawmaker's role, a new responsibility as the protector of people's interests. However, the new position of the Supreme Court could not be understood, and the Court & the House have had confrontations. Political activism sometimes often tends to become a legal and pro-rich conservatist act. It was not an unusual occurrence, and another interesting part of the judicial activism in India.

It was an evolving mechanism that was already being endorsed by the constitutions of democracies all over the world.

It has been regularly acknowledged that all three organs of the State must independently perform their respective functions, with no encroachment on the other two organs' functions. However, according to the society's interest as well as to harmonize the prevailing

36 John Gardner, Legal Positivism, 153 – 173, Alieen Kavanagh and John Oberdiek (Eds.), Arguing About Law (Routledge: Tylor and Francis Group, London and New York 2009)." 54 Basu, supra note 6

inconsistencies, Judges must have permission to go for reasonable ethical, moral, and rational considerations wherever required. The dynamic proportion to which the concept of judicial activism has manifested itself in the Indian judiciary makes it a suitable subject for comprehensive research in the vast legal field.

None of the accessed literature on constitutional law had specifically dealt with the concept of Judicial Activism and its impact on democratic dimensions of judicial institutions since its inception. A clear lacuna was perceived regarding whether or not the concept of judicial activism was imbibed in the Indian Constitution. There has been a functional creative mission to fulfil the security of fundamental rights as well as egalitarian aspiration of such a vast population.

Even literature and sources particularly related to the matter of Judicial Activism have not competently explored the issue: whether or not Judicial Activism has been instrumental in promoting the high benches for delivering vividly socialist announcements in citizen's interests under the Constitution's command.

2. CONCEPTION, DEFINITION, AND FORM OF JUDICIAL ACTIVISM

The term 'Judicial Activism' is utilized for the court's exceptional part, as it provides valuable conclusions, allowing assistance to persecuted person/persons, following its judicial, social, and moral sense, in situations wherein there exists silent statutory law or even contrary. Some jurists have also described it as "non-interpretive judicial review.[37]

We know that the British Constitution is unwritten, and the House is superior. The job of the courts is clearly to consider the laws. The courts should not alter and change the vocabulary of the constitutional laws, set down or add or subtract terms from them, for that affect the highest will of the Parliament.

Contrastingly, it is the Constitution that is paramount in countries that are having a written constitution, such as India and U.S.A. Since the courts must read the language of the Constitution, the judiciary in these countries have greater influence than its peers.

The judicial system in India occupies a significant place as it enquires about the validity, interpretation, and implementation of laws framed by the legislature. Besides the settlement of mutual disputes, the disputes arising out of clashes between Centre and State and amongst the States also fall under the domain of the judiciary. It protects the liberties as well as the rights of Indian citizens. Justice, which is fair and just to all without any discrimination is expected from the Judiciary. Moreover, the efficiency of the government largely depends on an impartial, independent, and positive justice. In performing its duties in terms of power as well as executive control, the Indian judiciary is fair as well as neutral. But in Indian socio-economic-political contexts, the demands from the judiciary are even greater. Injustice and analphabets are the obstacles in the way of ensuring dignity for all. The whole

---

37 Bachan Lal Kalgotra, Evolution And Jurisprudential Dimensions Of Judicial Activism, K. L. Bhatia (ed.), Judicial Activism & Social Change 242 (ISBN, India 1990)."

government structure is based on fair treatment for all. The social and economic nature of the judiciary is now being accepted worldwide.

Arthur M. Schlesinger was the first to use the term 'judicial activism' in an article on the United States' Supreme Court published in the Fortune magazine's January 1947 edition.[38] He used the phrase 'judicial activists' while referring to Justices Black, Rutledge, Murphy, and Douglas. He differentiated them from '*Champions of Self Restraint*' i.e., Frankfurter, Burton, and Jackson. In the article, Chief Justice Vinson with Justice Reed appeared above with the '*Balance of Power*' title. The article doesn't attempt to define the phrase 'judicial activist'. Schlesinger, however, tried to explain the tension between two parties in a way that concretes the meaning of his coined word. As the advocacy community saw, Supreme Court claimed that social security should be supported by it.

The 'Champions' defended a program of self-restraint by the courts. When one party viewed the court as a mechanism for obtaining the required social outcomes, the second saw it as a weapon to make for positive or bad results for the government's other branches.

Schlesinger understands the legal realism behind the Black/Douglas interpretation deriving from the idea that are particularly prevalent at 'Yale Law School', thereby characterizing the dispute. The Yale thesis, he outlined, is that deciding from outcome to cause is a matter of reverse engineering. In this sense, a prudent judge understands that political judgment is unavoidable, and he gives no pretence of objectivity and exercises judicial authority knowingly, taking into consideration social outcomes.[39]

Justice Samuel Alito's former law clerk, Keenan Kmiec, provides Judicial Activism the following *five core meanings*:

1. Withdrawal of other branches arguably Constitutional actions.
2. Failure in adhering to precedent.

38 Arthur M. Schlesinger Jr., The Supreme Court: 1947, Fortune magazine, Jan. 1947."

39 Keenan D. Kmiec, The Origin & Current Meanings of Judicial Activism, 92 Calif. Law Rev. 1441 (2004).

3. Judicial "legislation".
4. Variations from an acknowledged interpretive method.
5. Result-oriented judging.[40]

40 bid.

3. DEFINITION

Merriam Webster, defines Judicial Activism as "the practice in the judiciary of expanding and protecting individuals' rights through decisions that depart from the established precedent or are independent of or in opposition to supposed Constitutional or legislative intent."[41]

Black's Law Dictionary illustrates Judicial Activism as "a philosophy of judicial decision-making whereby judges allow their personal views around public policy, among other factors to guide their decisions; usually with suggestion that adherents of this philosophy tend to find Constitutional violations and are willing to ignore precedent."[42]

AS STATED BY JUSTICE J.S. VERMA:

"Judicial Activism must necessarily mean the active process of implementation of the rule of law essential for the preservation of a functional democracy."[43]

A.M. AHMADI, FORMER CHIEF JUSTICE OF INDIA STATED:

"Judicial Activism is a necessary adjunct of the judicial function from the protection of public interest, as opposed to private interest, happens to be its main concern."[44]

PROF. UPENDRA BAXI EXPRESSES:

"Judicial Activism is an ascriptive term. It means different things to different people. While some may exalt the term by describing it as judicial creativity, the dynamism of the judges, bringing a revolution in the field of human rights & social welfare through the enforcement of public duties, etc. Others have criticized the term by describing it as judicial extremism,

---

41 Merriam-Webster's, Dictionary of Law (Springfield, Massachusetts: Merriam-Webster, 1999).

42 Garner A. Bryan, Black's Law Dictionary (West Group Publication, 7th edn., 2002)."

43 Manika, Judicial Activism: A means for Attaining Good Governance, VII (3) NALSA, Nyaya Deep 117132, (July 2006).

44 Ahmadi, supra note 29.

judicial terrorism, judicial transgression into the domains of the other two organs of the state, negating the Constitutional spirit."[45]

AS STATED BY K.L. BHATIA:

"Judicial activism in India is a movement from personal injury to public concern by relaxing, expanding, and broadening the concept of locus standi. Judicial activism in India is a progressive movement from 'personal injury standing' to 'public concern standing' by allowing access to justice to pro bono public that is public-spirited individuals and organizations on behalf of 'lowly and lost' or 'underprivileged' or 'underdogs' or 'little men' who on account of constraints of money, ignorance, illiteracy has been bearing the pains of excesses without access to justice."[46]

AS STATED BY JUSTICE P.N. BHAGWATI:

"The judge infuses life with blood into dry skeleton provided by the legislature and creates a living organism appropriate and adequate to meet the needs of the society. The Indian judiciary has adopted an activist, goal-oriented approach in the matter of interpretation of fundamental rights. The judiciary has expanded the frontiers of fundamental rights and the process rewritten in some parts of the Constitution through a variety of techniques of judicial activism. The Supreme Court of India has undergone a radical change in the last several years and the principle is now being identified in the process of justice and acting as the last resort for the bewildered."[47]

AS STATED BY JUSTICE P.B. SAWANT:

"Judicial activism is a procedure to evolve new principles, concepts, maxims, formulae and relief to do justice or to expand the standing of the litigant

45 Manika, supra note 61.

46 K.L. Bhatia, judicial review & judicial activism - A comparative study of India and Germany from an Indian perspective 116 (Deep & Deep Publications, New Delhi, 1997)."

47 Justice P.N. Bhagwati, Enforcement of Fundamental rights – Role of the Courts 24 Indian Bar Review 19 (1997).

and open the door of courts for the needy or to entertain litigation affecting the entire society or a section of it – as in case of public interest litigation."[48]

The *'father of judicial activism'*, Lord Denning, has provided recommendations in search of the spirit of the British Constitution. He based his recommendations on three instincts:

"The instinct for justice, which he associates particularly with the independence of the judges and certainty of the law; the instinct for liberty which involves freedom of discussion, (including freedom of the press) and also freedom of association (including the right to form political parties); finally, a practical instinct which leads to a balancing of rights with duties, and powers with safeguards, so that neither rights nor powers shall be exceeded or abused."[49]

The concept of Judicial activism specifies determining a case in contradiction of the Constitution's plain meaning for promoting the political preferences of a judge. Further attempts have been made to provide other concepts worth considering. In litigation, a ruling can be referred to as 'activism' where the judge gives the ruling on issues not appropriate for the disposal of the dispute or where it implements State or federal laws.[50]

It has been argued by David A. Strauss that:

"Judicial Activism can be narrowly defined as one or more of three possible actions:

1. *Overturning laws as unconstitutional.*
2. *Overturning judicial precedent; and*
3. *Ruling against a preferred interpretation of the Constitution."*[51]

48 P.B. Sawant, Judicial Independence – Myth and Reality 70 (Board of Extra Mural Studies, Pune, 1987).

49 Lord Denning, Changing Law, Edward Mac Whinney (ed.), Judicial Review 17 (University of Toronto Press, Toronto, 4th edn., 1965).

50 Kermit Roosevelt II, The Myth Of Judicial Activism 38-39 (Universal Law Publishing Co. Pvt. Ltd, New Delhi, 2011)."

51 Wikipedia, *supra* note 67 and http://wwwlawteacher.net/free-law-essays/Constitutional-law/judicial-activism-is-a-term-law-essays.php

4. JUDICIAL ACTIVISM: AN INHERENT POWER OF JUDICIAL REVIEW

Judicial activism is widely established in Bangladesh, Canada, Pakistan, New Zealand, South Africa, Sri Lanka, Australia, and England. It originated from England, with the court reviewing the executive's acts for ensuring that they act within their competence's limits described by the parliamentary statutes.

The courts in England have strengthened their jurisdiction through the interpretation process. The executives are imposed with great limitations through gradually subjecting their acts to the principles of natural justice, analytically analysing the exercise of discretionary powers,[52] as well as the decisions of a certain authority that are constructed narrowly by the administrative tribunals that are final as well as conclusive.[53]

Thus, in England, the administrative action was judicially reviewed although the courts could not revise the actions of the Parliament since it was the supreme body. The principle of parliamentary sovereignty[54] by Professor Dicey was a British legislative embodiment of Austin's sovereignty theory. The poor profile of England's judicial position corresponded in principle to the sovereignty of Parliament. However, the innovative attempt taken by the judiciary to defend democracy and reinforce the rule of law was the reasoning for such a self-rejection.

JUDICIAL REVIEW MODELS

Following are the models that are considered for judicial review:

- 'Technocratic model' – judges merely act as technocrats and could hold a law as invalid when legislative powers are ultra vires.

52 Padfield v. Minister of Agriculture, Fisheries and Food (1968) AC 997: (1968) 1 All ER 694.

53 Anisminic Ltd. V. Foreign Compensation Commission (1962) 2 AC 147: (1969) 1 All ER 208.

54 A. V. Dicey & E. C. S. Wade, Introduction To The Study Of The Law Of The Constitution (Macmillan & Co., London 1952).

- 'liberal model' – The Constitution's provisions are substantially interpreted by the court, keeping the Constitution up to date with its dynamic interpretations.

A court that gives new meanings to constitutional provisions, to enhance the varying socio-economic conditions, or increasing the horizons of an individual's rights is considered as an 'activist court'.

CONCEPT OF JUDICIAL PASSIVISM AND ACTIVISM

Judicial activism can either be negative or positive. A court utilizing its ingenuity for maintaining the present circumstances in power relations is considered as 'negatively activist' whereas; a court involved in modifying the power relation, for making them more reasonable is considered as 'positively activist'.[55] The U.S. Supreme Court's decision in *Dred Scott v. New York*[56] is an example of negative judicial activism, however; the same court's decision in *Brown v. Board of Education*[57] is an example of positive judicial activism.

In *Dred Scott*, the U.S. Supreme Court endorsed slavery as being protected by the right to property and in *Lochner v. New York*, it held a law against children employment as violative of the due process clause of the Constitution.

Judicial activism and *judicial passivism* are constantly competing as opposite theories of judicial attitude, towards the construction of the statutes. Contrastingly, there also exist various arguments in against of both these standards.

The principle of 'judicial passivism' is mainly based on the 'separation of power' theory as well as on declaration of 'judicial functions' theory that assigned the position & the role of courts in stating what the law is (*jus dicere*). Many who support this school do not move beyond written rules, since they think *written what is meant and meant what is written – ita scriptum est* (it is so written), even if a literal reading of laws leads to absurdity, suffering, or inequality. They are further against

55 *Ibid.*

56 Dred Scott v. Stanford 60 U.S. 393 (1856)

57 347 U.S. 483 (1954)

the awarding of discretionary jurisdictions and Lord Camden clarifies the authority of a judge:

"Is the law of tyrants – always unknown, different in different men, causal and depending on Constitution, temper, and passion – and that is the best it is often caprice, while in the worst it is every vice, folly, and passion."[58]

It is also referred to as the administrative tradition where judges persistently stuck to the written text considered as '*ex-cathedra*'.

In contrast, judicial activism finds its origins in the idea of bringing justice to the final intent of any statute, even if it tantamount to defeating the very ambition for which legislation was passed. Judicial advocacy then reflects Nigeria's leading lawyer, B.O. Okere's words as:

"Constitutive in theory, liberal in conception and teleological in essence"[59]

Such tradition originates from the political whiggism that insists judges to analyse social concepts and view them in a manner suitable to the ends of social justice. If a judge doesn't take the literal significance of the statute as active, but it does what is congruent in its judgment with the law spirit, it is known as an activist.

THEORIES OF JUDICIAL REVIEW

There have been various hypotheses about the judicial exercise of the interpretative authority. The spectrum varied from non-interpretivism to interpretivism. Among these, there exists structuralism, non-originalism, originalism, intentionalism, textualism, etc.[60]

---

58 L. P. Goldberg and E. Levenson, Lawless Judges 339 (The Rand School Press, New York, 1935); Clement James Dakas, Poverty and Tyranny of Judicial Passivism: Imperative of Judicial Activism in Nigeria JILI (April-Dec. 1997).

59 B. O. Okere, Judicial activism or passivity in interpreting the Nigerian Constitution, in E. I. Nwogugu (Ed.), Current Legal Problems In Nigeria: Proceedings Of The Anambra State Law Conference 43 (Fourth Dimension Publications Ltd., Enugu, Nigeri, 1988).

60 Ibid.

TEXTUALISM

It is the outcome of frequent shifts in the approach to the simple meaning. Thurgood Marshall J, preferred to read documents, and articulated his opinion, while the Court will not enable a true reading of the Law to contribute to preposterous consequences, it deferred to the authority of the parliament and agreed with the congressmen typical of the language of a bill, we usually believe 'that most of the Congressmen are voting on the language of a bill.'

The textualists emphasize on the rule of plain meaning without the use of any legislative intent and legislative history. In *Immigration and Naturalization Service v. Cardozo-Fonseca*[61], Scalia J clearly stated that:

"Where language is clear we are not free to replace it with an unenacted legislative intent."[62]

Situations where textualism does not work are those where there exists open worded laws and not so clear terms used in any acts our Constitution. For instance, 'Constitutional amendment', 'failure of Constitutional machinery' (the government of the State cease to carry on), 'consultation', 'privileges and immunities', 'equality before the law', 'public interest', 'life or personal liberty', 'reasonable restrictions', 'educationally and socially backward classes', etc.[63]

INTENTIONALISM

This needs both 'extrinsic' as well as 'intrinsic' aids in determining the intentions of those who framed the statute. One end of Intentionalism is textualism because this also needs determining the original intention through the interpretation of the language that is utilized in the statute. It has been stated by Felix Frankfurter J once:

"That a court's task is to construe not English but congressional English"[64]

As stated by Reid J:

---

61 94 L Ed 2d 434: 480 US 421 (1986).

62 *Id.* at 453.

63 Anirudh Prasad & C.P. Singh, Judicial Power & Judicial Review 167 (Eastern Book Company, Lucknow, First edn., 2012).

64 Ibid.

"In the interpretation of statutes, the function of the court is easily stated. It is to construe the language to give effect to the intent of Congress. There is no invariable rule for the discovery of that intention."[65]

ORIGINALISM

Originalists put stress upon the original intention of the Constitutional framers to look at the text of the law itself and, where the wording is not plain. Originalists contend against judicial ingenuity and claim that if framers' text and purpose were not enough to assign sense to a constitutional clause; judges should show restraint and not use such a law to obstruct acts performed by legislation and executives in the political branches[66]. Originalists contend, that a particular activity, or actions, can be considered unconstitutional only when it is entirely apparent from the constitutional document or the purposes of the framers. Judicial evaluation is narrow although lesser intense than the textualists.[67]

It has been stated by Goldsworthy that for three reasons moderate originalism is superior to its extreme versions as well as differs from it as:

- It is appropriate, though not and any other proof that evidence of the purpose of the framers was readily accessible to their potential audience at the time of the Constitution's enforcement.
- The founding father's enactment intentions are relevant to the meaning of the constitution and not their application intentions.
- Where relevant proof of the purpose of framers does not settle a conflict, then judges will be obliged to rule with imagination and to stipulate the importance of the challenged clause after having considered concerns like public policies and justice, coherence with general principles and legal doctrines.

---

65 H. Levi, An Introduction to Legal Reasoning 15 U. Chi. L. Rev. 501, 520-23 (1948).

66 Christopher N. May and Allan Ides, Constitutional Law – National Power and Federalism: Examples and Explanations 36 (Aspen publishers, New York, 3rd edn., 2004).

67 Ibid.

NON-ORIGINALISM

There are two types of non-originalists[68]:

First – They are closer to textualists who argue that the original terms of the document itself are the sole valid ground for reading the Constitution. The textualists, as well as legal experts, are close to one another.

Second – The interpreters of the Constitution give greater rights to non-originalists. They recognize that while courts should use both the text & the motives of the framers, these references do not restrict them.

The most extensive factor for non-originalists was the weakness of a judge's authority for judicial review in absence of any evident support from the constitutional document as well as its purposes.

STRUCTURALISM

They collected the interpretation principle, not from words of a single passage, but from the framework or structure of the Constitution.[69] Furthermore, the following three structural principles are the guiding spirit for interpretations of a constitution as envisaged by the concept of structuralism:

- a written Constitution.
- separation of powers among the government's three branches (Judiciary, executive and legislature)[70].
- Federalism (a division of power among the federating States and the Central Government).[71]

Both independent sources, as well as textual provisions, are utilized by structuralists for searching out the meaning.[72]

68 *Supra* note 67

69 *Ibid*

70 *Prasad. Supra* note 64

71 *Ibid.*

72 Antonin Scalia J., Originalism: The Lesser Evil, 57 U. Chi. L. Rev. 849, 862 (1989).

- *Keshavananda Bharti v. State of Kerala*[73] is an exceptional example for structuralism, where it has been ruled by the majority that the Constitution cannot be amended by the Parliament to modify its basic structure. For breaching the separation of powers, Supreme Court found the Constitutional (39th Amendment) Act, 1975 to be unconstitutional.[74]

- In *Maneka Gandhi v. Union of India*[75], the structural-based approach was reaffirmed when Articles 14, 19 and 21 were observed to be considered together to make process fair and right (*the golden triangle*).

- In *I.R. Coelho v. the State of T.N.*, the Supreme Court's nine judge Bench considered that:

- *"When this triangle of Article 21 read with Article 14 and Article 19 is sought to be eliminated, not only the 'essence of right' test but also the 'rights test' has to apply."*

Various hypotheses surrounding the exercise of judicial authority indicate that the two sides of the judicial action of the court are *activism* and *restraint*. However, nobody should pretend to be adequate to fix all of life's problems. To explain this, the notion of the judiciary - self-reduced or legalism, reiterates the simplistic notion such that there is already an entirely fixed "right-responding" solution to some procedural issue in the pre-existing body of definitive legal documents (in fact, the constitutional text as well as its deterioration, which provide an interpretive precedent).[76]

There always exists a struggle among two concepts 'self-restraint or conservatism', and 'activism or non-originalism or liberalism'. No judge can be *a hundred percent* an activist or restraints.

---

73 (1973) 4 SCC 225: AIR 1973 SC 1461."

74 Supp SCC 1: AIR 1975 SC 2299."

75 (1978) 1 SCC 248: 1978 AIR 597(SC).

76 Anthony Blackshield & George Williams, Australian Constitutional Law and Theory 328 (The Federation Press, Australia, 2006)."

JUDICIAL ACTIVISM VERSUS SEPARATION OF POWERS

The ultimate purpose of our Constitution, as set out in the preamble by its founding fathers, is to secure a 'welfare state'. By now, the three constitutional institutions have also been established to achieve this objective. The Indian Constitution does not expressly provide for the doctrine of separation of powers but in *Asif Hameed and Ors. v. State of J&K,*[77] the roles of the various government sections were properly distinguished where the Supreme Court noted:

"No organ can usurp the function assigned to another. The only check on our exercise of power is the self-imposed discipline of judicial restraint."

The Constitution's fundamental design relies on the principle of separation of powers, with the presence of checks and balances. The organizational domains of these three major organs cannot be difficult to discern conceptually, however, the judicial activism's real concern is its permissible boundaries.

The Supreme Court in *Union of India v. Deoki Nandan Agarwal*[78] put forth a view that legislature cannot be directed for making a specific law by the court.

Similarly, in *Rajindera Singh v. Prem Mai and Ors*[79], it refers to a pretext sometimes provided by the court for legitimate violation of the executive or legislature jurisdiction (in situations when the other two institutions do not do the job properly); as a dupe argument may be made against the courts (since for half a century there are pending cases in courts).

Although, practically during the time of delivering justice, there are situations that require removing some legislative gap or modification of an executive order. In these circumstances, the court might find itself passing decisions related to policy making, partaking the character of a political decision maker.[80] Additionally, there is always the complexity

77 AIR 1989 SC 1899 (para 17- 19)

78 AIR 1992 SC 96.

79 2007 [11] SCC 37

80 Prof. Virendra Kumar, Judges v. Judges, The Tribune (New Delhi), Dec. 21, 2007.

of balancing the separation of powers and judicial activism in such situations.[81]

The Indian Supreme Court has now started looking above the social and economic protection of the downtrodden, and gradually progressing towards including topics from the realm of public administration. For instance:

- In 2006, some guidelines were issued by Supreme Court for reforming the police administration.

- Also, in legislative spheres gradually similar guidelines were issued.

It is on account of such interventions by the court that, issues like sexual harassment at workplace have been able to find their platform for discussion and subsequently a formal set of rules and mandates based on the conclusions.[82] Similarly, the procedures that must be followed by a police officer before an arrest, (often compared with the American Miranda Rights) which can be called the 'Basu Rights' in India are in fact result of judicial intervention.[83]

Judicial activism is a concept of immense proportions and not just a phrase. The numerous definitions and meanings offered by lawyers only helps us to reveal its underlying layers.

Judicial activism has never been a straitjacket formula. In terms of shape, time, and origins of its existence, it has changed from one constitutional era to another. It was the Rule of Law in line with one Constitution and the preamble under another. It was the Bill of Rights under one Constitution, and the federalism under a different Constitution. Justice advocacy must be to defend people from the unconstitutional invasion of their constitutional rights and equality by the State.

---

81 Surat Singh, Judicial Activism – How Wise, How Otherwise, K. Mahesh Bishwajit Bhattacharyya (ed.), Judging the Judges 141-142 (Gyan Publishing House, New Delhi, 1999).

82 Vishaka v. State of Rajasthan, AIR 1997 SC 3014.

83 D.K. Basu v. State of W.B., (1993) 2 SCC 746.

5. HISTORICAL PERSPECTIVE OF JUDICIAL ACTIVISM

ORIGIN

While the fundamental controversy on Judicial Activism has been making rounds since Bentham (that stated it as '*miserable sophistry*') and Blackstone days (that advocated '*judicial legislation*'), somewhere in the 20th century the word formally came into presence for characterizing the act of judicial legislation which means '*judges making positive rules.*'[84]

In India, the Regulatory Act, 1773, the first Constitution for India to be framed by the British Parliament, was the new idea of the communication between the East India Company & the Crown of England. In Bengal, the Act constituted the Supreme Council of four councillors and the Governor-General. *The CEO* of the other two provinces, Madras and Bombay, were named. A Supreme Court, composed of a Chief Justice and three judges, was also created. The governing legislation didn't clearly define the duties of the Supreme Court, and this led to a fierce confrontation; the Supreme Council denounced the concurrent governance of the judges.

Criticizing the spirit of encroachment of the judges, a 1781 document recites:

"They have subjected every zamindar in the country to their jurisdiction. They have granted writs of ejectment against persons who have bought estates by the order of the Governor-General and Council. They have ordered a writ of habeas corpus against the Naib Subha who will have executed it, to avoid the consequences of such a measure, entreated the Chief Justice to suspend the execution of the writ."[85]

---

84 Brian Bix, Positively Positivism, 85 VALR 889-907 (1999) (book review) cited from Keenan D. Kmiec, The Origin & Current Meanings of Judicial Activism, 92 CALIF LR 1441 (2004).

85 Henry Dodwell (Ed.), Warren Hastings' Letters to Sir John Macpherson 72 (Faber & Gwyer, London, 1927)

The disagreement among Court & the Council extended in a horrendous proportion, which threatened the lifetime relationship between Chief Justice Sir Elijah Impey and Warren Hastings. In May of 1780, Impey complained that marriage among Philip and Hastings Francis had been sacrificed. Although, Hastings efficiently appealed to the Chief Justice for granting him authority over the district court's administration.

In all British colonies, including India, judicial review of constitutional acts was in its early stages, as colonial assemblies were still inheriting their authority from the laws passed by the British Parliament. It was the Government of India Act 1858, where the jurisdiction of the British Parliament to judicially review legislation was exercised by the Indian courts.

The judicial review principle was introduced by Calcutta High Court in the following words:

"The theory of every government with a written Constitution forming the fundamental and the paramount law of the nation must be that an Act of legislature. If void, it cannot bind the courts, and oblige them to give it effect; for this would be to overthrow in fact what was established in theory which makes that operative in law, which was not law."[86]

In the appraisal of Indian judicial history, which displays knowledge about the judgment of the Crown's courts and the Company's courts in colonial India, an assessment of which indicates that the outline of the judicial activism was clear, even during the period of the pre-independence colonial era.

The Council held in *Emperor v. Sibnath Banerji*[87] that the Court was willing, according to the Government of India Act (1935) Section 59 (2), to examine the legitimacy of the orders passed. However, the Privy Council's judicial investigation concluded with the dissolution of the Privy Council Competence Statute on 10 October 1949.

86 Empress v. Burah and Book Singh, I.L.R. 3 Cal. 63, 87-88 (1878)." 116 AIR (32) 1945 PC 156.

87 AIR (32) 1945 PC 156

A further case wherein the Privy Council contained the 'equal chance to hear' principles under meaning of Government of India Act of, 1935 Section 240 (3) was the *Commissioner for India v. I.M. Hall.*[88]

Another example to note here is that of the Federal Court when adjudicating in *Niharendu Dutt Majumdar v. Emperor* according to the Indian Government Act, 1935[89]. The court observed that mere critique of the government or even mockery, is no sedition unless the act is determined to destroy regard for the government and to ensure that citizens cease obedience to the crown and allow only anarchy to replace it.

The Federal Court, nevertheless, was solely a literal translator under the Government of India Act, 1935. It was unguided about the rights, and the Executive had comprehensive discharge.

'Indian Judicial Activism' can be divided into the following periods or eras for making its historical study simpler:

1. Pre–emergency era (1950 – 1974)

– The Nehru era (1950 – 1964)

– Post–Nehru era (1965 – 1974)

2. Emergency era (1975 – 1977)
3. Post–emergency era (1978 onwards)

PRE-EMERGENCY ERA (1950 – 1974)

In 1934, the concept of an Indian Constituent Assembly was recommended by M. N. Roy, a pioneer of the Indian Communist movement and an advocate of radical democracy. Finally, the demands of independence were put forth by Indian National Congress in 1935 which was eventually promised to be handed over by in 1940.

The Indian National Congress in 1935 demanded independence and Britain decided to give it over in 1940. The Constitution of India may have come into force in 1950 but it wouldn't be wrong to say that it matured over more than 2 centuries until independence. And it is

88 AIR (35) 1948 PC 121, para 21 and 22.
89 AIR 1942 FC 22."

only expanding with each passing day. These are devised laws based on the debates and conversations in the constituent assembly.

Honourable Shri N.V. Gadgil, during his Constituent Assembly debate speech, focused on those five points of views relevant to examine the modern Constitution:[90]

- The nature of the State for which the Constitution is created
- The nature of the Constitution itself
- The nature of Legislature
- The nature of the Executive
- The nature of the Judiciary

Only a thorough analysis of the text of our Constitution and deliberations at the Constituent Assembly reveal the high degree of concern that the framers had displayed in judicial affairs, with the powers of the Supreme Court in mind. In their view, a single centralized judiciary and a uniform code of laws were necessary to preserve the country's stability. The Indian judiciary made considerable efforts to follow the double principles of the Legislature and the Judiciary. However, some of the assemblymen considered that the legislature should receive the final say in some aspects of the social movement. In these matters, the judges believe that the best way to read the law in writing is to have a restricted position.

THE NEHRU ERA (1950 – 1964)

India's first Prime Minister, Pt. Jawaharlal Nehru believed in providing the judiciary a restrictive position when interpreting the legislations enacted by the Parliament. He can be quoted from his Constituent Assembly debates that:

"No Supreme Court and no judiciary can stand in judgment over sovereign will of the Parliament representing the will of the entire community. If we go wrong here and there, it can point it out but in the ultimate analysis,

90 C. A. D. Proceedings (Vol. XI), Friday, Nov. 18, 1949.

where the future of the community is concerned, no judiciary can come in the way."[91]

Talking about the right to property, he categorically emphasized:

"Within limits, no judge and no Supreme Court can made itself a third chamber of the legislature."[92]

Shri Alladi Krishnaswamy Ayyer, a significant contributor in the drafting of the Constitution expressed in relation to the Judiciary that:

"While there can be no two opinions about the mandate of judicial independence, it is also necessary to keep in view that the doctrine of independence is not to be raised to the level of dogma, to enable the judiciary to function as a kind of super-legislative or super-executive. The judiciary is there to interpret the law or adjudicate upon rights."[93]

Dr. Ambedkar observes:

"We are therefore placed in two difficult positions. One is to give the judiciary the authority to sit in judgment over the will of the legislature and to question the law made by the legislature on the ground that it is not good law, in consonance with fundamental principles. Is that a desirable principle?

The second position is that the legislature ought to be trusted not to make bad laws. It is very difficult to come to any definite conclusion. There are dangers on both sides. For myself, I cannot altogether omit to the possibility of a Legislature packed by party-men making laws that may abrogate or violate what we regard as certain fundamental principle affecting the life and liberty of an individual. At the same time, I do not see how five or six gentlemen sitting in the Federal or Supreme Court examining laws made by the Legislature and by dint of their conscience or their bias or their prejudices are to be trusted to determine which law is good and which law is bad."[94]

91 Rajeev Dhavan, Nehru, Law and Social Change, Rajeev Dhavan & Thomas Paul, (Eds.), Nehru and The Constitution 55 (Indian Law Institute, New Delhi, 1992).

92 B. Shiva Rao, The Framing of India's Constitution: A Study, 5 Indian Institute of Public Administration, New Delhi 235 (1968).

93 Alladi Krishnaswamy Ayyar, C. A. D. (Vol. XI), 837, Nov. 23, 1949

94 C. A. D. Proceedings (Vol.VII), 1000, Nov. 1948.

He further adds:

"The Constituent Assembly in making a constitution has no partisan motive. Beyond securing a good and workable Constitution it has no axe to grind. In considering the Articles of the Constitution it has no eye on getting through that measure. The future Parliament, if it met as a Constituent Assembly, its members will be acting as partisans seeking to carry amendment to the Constitution to facilitate the passing of party measures that they have failed to get through Parliament because of some Article of the Constitution which has acted as an obstacle in their way. Parliament will have an axe to grind while to the Constituent Assembly has none. That is difference between Constituent Assembly and the future Parliament. That explains why to the Constituent Assembly though elected on the limited franchise can be trusted to pass the Constitution by a simple majority & why the Parliament though elected on adult suffrage cannot be trusted along the same power to amend it."[95]

A fully independent judicial body that is often a victim of executive's scepticism, is not an unusual sight. The fear is that, as a third legislative body, the court can put itself above regulation. However, not just lawmakers but courts tended to be under the dominion of legislative dominance during the Nehruvian period.

Since S.P. Sathe has precisely stated:

"The judges of the Supreme Court have been brought up in the English positivist tradition and were reluctant to assume wider power for the Court. Both, leaders of the Constituent Assembly and the judges shared a similar perception at the beginning. There didn't seem to be much dispute about technocrat nature of the judiciary that only responds to legal queries. Therefore, it was easy for the political establishment to manage the Court. It simply amended the Constitution and asked the Court to respond to it."[96]

Generally, there are three reasons for such judicial passivism:

- Firstly, the judges from the Nehruvian era were drawn from the pool appointed during the colonial regime. These judges

95 *Id* at 43-44
96 *Sathe. Supra* at 21

strongly believed in the sovereignty of the Parliament like how it was during the colonial control in India.

- Secondly, the courts of the Nehruvian period accepted that law was proclaimed by Parliament and that it was the responsibility of the courts to view and maintain the law as it is. This legitimate passivity is dependent on the Anglo-Saxon tradition affirming that: "a judge does not make law; he merely interprets. Law is existing and eminent; the judge merely finds it. He merely reflects what legislature has said." It is the judicial function's '*photographic theory*'.[97]

- Thirdly, parliamentarians of the Nehruvian period were men of peace and dignity. They were the leaders who joined in the national campaign for independence and thus wore the sacrificial halo. Politicians enjoyed even more prestige compared to judges.[98]

Politicians from the Nehruvian period were not only admired by the people but also by the courts. Subsequently, legal contention was practiced by the judiciary to invalidate Parliament's constitutional actions.

The conflict between the Supreme Court & the Parliament started right after the independence, as the elected representatives emphasized their mandate to mould the nation's future. It was a republic. But the judiciary was almost as ardent in not seeking to interfere with its independence either within the government or the legislature as it can be seen from what Madhukar Hiralal Kania, then the Chief Justice of India, stated on 28 February 1950 at the inauguration of the Supreme Court of India:

"That judiciary must be quite untouchable by the legislature or executive authority in the performance of its duties."

---

97 Chief Justice P.N. Bhagwati, Judicial Activism in India, (available at: https://media.law.wisc.edu/m/4mdd4/gargoyle_17_1_3.pdf)

98 Ibid.

From 1950 onwards, judicial activism became obvious in India.

The Supreme Court's activist decisions in *Champakam Dorairajan v. State of Madras*[99], *Brij Bhushan v. State of Delhi*[100], and *Romesh Thappar v. State of Madras*[101] invalidating the laws issued by the Parliament resulted in chaos in the Constitutional system.

The Constitution (Amendment) Act of 1951 was then enacted by Parliament to address the judgment delivered in *Champakam Dorairajan* by the Madras High Court & later by the Supreme Court of India. It made several changes to the provisions related to fundamental rights and provided means to restrict freedom of speech and expression. These changes were made to show the legislative dominance over the judiciary.

The Supreme Court dealt with its Judicial Review's first case in *A.K. Gopalan v. Madras.*[102] A *habeas corpus* writ against the preventive arrest of Communist leader A.K. Gopalan raised the first major constitutional matter. The argument was that whether there was a breach of its human rights disguised by the terms of the Preventive Detention Act of 1950 (Article 13, 19, 21, and 22). The lawyer on behalf of the petitioner argued that freedom to travel was a constitutional right under Article 19 and that the prosecution counsel had to show that preventive detention was a reasonable restriction in compliance with Article 19 (5) clause (2). The concern was whether imprisonment of anyone should be justified solely because it was done 'following the legal procedure' as set down in Article 21 of the Constitution. Otherwise, it would only be true if it complied with natural justice standards, such as hearing the individual involved.

The Supreme Court took narrow view of Article 21 in the *A. K. Gopalan* case as well as declined to consider whether there were any defects in the proceedings set down by statute. It was held that 'legal procedure' varies from that given by the 14th Amendment to the American Constitution on 'substantial due process.' It was suggested

99 AIR 1951 SC 226.
100 AIR 1950 SC 129.
101 AIR 1950 SC 124.
102 AIR 1950 SC 27.

that the framers of the Indian Constitution intentionally used the former definition rather than the latter. For many years the narrow construction of Article 21 persisted.

In his judicial analysis, Professor Edward Mc Whinney claimed that a strongly optimistic stance towards constitutional interpretation had been taken by the Supreme Court of India. The Professor forecasted the following:

"It seems like that the Indian Constitution will be subjected to some stress and strain in the future unless the Indian Supreme Court is prepared to adopt a more consciously creative role."[103]

Green, an English columnist noticed that Supreme Court of India had not differed from the deep-rooted legal principles of England.[104] He said, that in England, they denied that they were making legislation for a long time. The custom of the English court was to read the terms in that as well as not to interpret the extrajudicial truth.

This is referred to as legal positivism, described by Dworkin as:

"A theory which holds the truth of legal propositions consists in facts about rules that has been adopted by specific social institutions, and in nothing else."[105]

In the following terms, Dr. Rajeev Dhavan identified the convention of 'black letter law' that leads to legal positivism:[106]

"The 'black letter law' convention seeks to interpret the law as a distinct, relatively autonomous reality. Within this tradition, 'law' is separated from morality. It is understood and interpreted by obscure rules known only to the initiated and critiqued based on self-constituted legal principles and concepts."

---

103 Edward McWhinney, Judicial Review 139 (University of Toronto Press, 4thedn., 1969).

104 Green, 'Preventive Detention Act' 44 Indian Law Review 304, 309 (1950)."

105 "Ronald M. Dworkin, Taking Rights Seriously (Gerald Duckworth and Co.,United States, 1977)."

106 Rajiv Dhavan Introduction to (ed.), Marc Galanter, Law and Society in Modern India (Law in India Series, Oxford University Press, 1997).

The interpretative approach of the Supreme Court of India in *Gopalan* is positivist since the

Court has declined to assign a general meaning to the terms 'procedure established by law' or 'personal liberty' as mentioned in Article 21. A court is said to have progressed towards Judicial Activism when it represents the theory of law that identifies a statute not only as it is, but also as it should be.[107]

In *Gopalan*, the opposing opinion of Justice Fazl Ali showed that the activism of the Supreme Court was a seed for the judicial aspect of its legislative function from very first year of its inception. While Nehru deeply believed in the independence of the judiciary, he nevertheless claimed on 16 May 1951 in the Lok Sabha, in no ambiguous terms, that Judiciary played no part in great schemes and significant social reforms. In his speech on the fourth amendment, he affirmed that it was unlikely for the judicial authority to rule on the high level of political, social, and economic issues and any of those matters that are beyond Judiciary's domain. So, in a way, he attempted to describe the perimeter of a judge that could not be crossed.

In *Romesh Thapar v State of Madras*[108], a petition, through the petitioner, was filed under Article 32 of the Constitution, challenging the Madras Government's order, banning the admission and dissemination of the weekly magazine viz 'Crossroads' printed and distributed in Bombay. In Madras, a restoration order was issued under Public Order Act of 1949. The Court rules that prohibition was a breach of the freedom of expression. The Parliament responded that the "public order" protection as a justification for enforcing limits on freedom of speech was provided for by the Constitution of India (Amendment) Act, 1951.

In *State of Madras v. Champakam Dorairajan*[109], the Court took a strict approach. Access to a medical university in State of Madras (presently called Tamil Nadu) was controlled by an order of the then popular government which categorized the total seats based on

107 Ibid.
108 AIR 1950 SC 124
109 AIR 1951 SC 226

community. While striking down the common order, the Court held that seats in an educational institution couldn't be distributed on community basis in the light of a strong worded Article 15(2). It was argued that the allocation of seats in favour of such a weaker group had constitutional significance because the guideline theory of government policy as mentioned in Article 46, empowered the State for promoting with special consideration the economic & educational interests of the weaker sections of the population recognised as the Scheduled Castes & the Scheduled Tribes. Although denying that, Court acknowledged that the Directive Principles of State Policy *"have to conform to and run as subsidiary to the chapter of Fundamental Rights."*

As early as 1951 in *Shankari Prasad Singh Deo v. Union of India*[110], the matter of allowing the amendment according to Article 368 of the Constitution, of the constitutional rights guaranteed by Part III, came before the Supreme Court. In this case the incorporation of Articles 31-A and 31-B was questioned in view of the supremacy of the statute of the Constitution (First Amendment) Act of 1951. Amongst other aspects, it was argued that since Article 13(2) prohibited legislation that was abridging fundamental rights, such an amendment prevented this abridgment because an amendment was still the law. The Court, dismissing its contention, held that Article 368 included the power to amend the constitution, including fundamental rights, and that in Article 13(2), the term "law" did not incorporate a constitutional amendment which was made in the exercise of the constituent power and not the legislative power.

Supreme Court and the Parliament have contradicted their understanding of the right to property clauses. While the Constituent Assembly took every step to discourage judicial intervention in the program of economic reforms practiced by the Congress Party after the days of the independence, the laws complimentary to the improvements in the property affairs were found unconstitutional by courts. The legality of such laws cannot be questioned under paragraphs (4) and (6) of Article 31 because of their supposed violation as per the provisions

110 AIR 1951 SC 458: 1952 SCR 89.

of Article 31. It was alleged that they have violated the right to equality guaranteed under Article 14 of the Constitution.

The Bihar Land Reforms Act, 1950 was brought into question in *Kameshwar Singh v. the State of Bihar.*[111] This piece of law was considered by the Patna High Court to be in breach of Article 14 of the Constitution. It reinforced the objection that differential compensation rates offered by the legislation on land reform were unfair, whereby compensation rates tapered as the land value increased. Though by amending the Constitution, the Parliament replied to this decision; adopting the process laid down in Article 368. The Constitution (First Amendment) Act, 1951 contained two new Sections, 31-A and 32-B, both aimed at excluding the judicial scrutiny of certain types of legislation which, resulting from suspected violations of certain constitutional rights, and those that eliminated certain types of interests in property. The first amendment that came into effect on 18 June 1951, further added a 'Ninth Schedule' to the Constitution. Any law inserted in it cannot be covered by the judicial review of the courts. Article 31-A exempted legislation on the elimination, concerning the right to equality mentioned in Article 14, right to different liberties mentioned in Article 19, and the right to property provided in Article 31 from the judicial scrutiny. Article 31-A, in the light of some of the constitutional rights provided by Part-III of the Constitution, along with Article 31B gave the laws of Ninth Schedule, immunity from being questioned.

It has been observed by a five-judge bench of the Supreme Court in *Ameerunnissa Begum v. Mahboob Begum*[112] that:

"A legislature which must, of necessity, have the power of making special laws to attain appropriate objects must have large powers of selection or classification of person and things upon which such rule is to operate. Hence, mere differentiation or inequality of treatment does not per se amount to discrimination."[113]

111 AIR 1951 Para 91
112 AIR 1953 SC 91.
113 Id at para 11.

In *Bela Banerjee* case[114], in Calcutta, a suit was brought before English Court to contest the authority of the Government to purchase land for the providing housing to refugees of East Pakistan. The Supreme Court observed that the fee owed for the purchase of land in exercise of eminent domain authority must be proportional to its market value. Nehru proposed amendments to the provision to amend laws regarding the elimination and nationalization of property owned by a zamindar, as well as regulation and order, and subversive practices in its social policy that had been put at risk. The chief ministers have been told by Nehru that the position of the justice system cannot be challenged:

"But if the Constitution itself comes in our way, then surely it is time to change that Constitution"[115]

The court held in *re State of West Bengal v Subodh Gopal Bose and Ors*[116], that an owner must be compensated even if the land was not covered in the state policy but was regulated or its use was reduced, causing the owner to be deprived of property. According to the Constitution (Fourth Amendment) Act, 1955, the assessment of just and fair compensation was removed from the purview of judicial review.

In *re K. K. Kochuni v. The State of Madras*[117], the Supreme Court neutralized the effects of those Constitutional reforms. It stated that any legislation that contributes to deprivation of property must stand the test of Article 19(5) that requires the freedom to possess, own, and dispose of property and is to be put under 'reasonable restrictions.'

Over the years, several changes to Article 31 were made that were subsequently withdrawn. The right to land, in other words, was provided for in two provisions in the Constitution: Article 19 (1)(f) and Article 31.[118] Post their modifications and omissions, we have not

---

114 State of W.B. v. Bela Banerjee, AIR 1954 SC 170."

115 Madhavi G. Divan, Judicial review: Supremacy of the Courts or of the Constitution 10 SCC J. 23-27 (2009).

116 AIR 1954 SC 92.

117 AIR 1960 SC 1080

118 The Constitution (Forty-fourth Amendment) Act, 1978, Acts of Parliament, 1978.

experienced judicial activism on right to land, following the omission of Article 31 from the list of constitutional rights.

However, by the late 1950s, the Court began considering its constitutional role at a significant dimension.

Justice Subba Rao (as he was then) held in *Basheshar Nath v Commissioner, Income Tax* that people cannot even waive their basic rights voluntarily. The learned Judge embraced such a suggestion by describing, in the following words, the position of the Court in a constructive way:[119]

"A large majority of our people is economically poor, educationally backward, and politically not yet conscious of their rights. Individually or even collectively, they cannot be pitted against State organizations and institutions, nor can they meet them on equal terms. In such circumstances, this court must protect their rights against themselves."

It truly marked the commencement of 'pro-poor judicial activism' in India.

It has been observed by the Mysore High Court's Division Bench in *Ramkrishna Singh v State of Mysore*[120] that:

"The decision of the Government that certain classes are 'socially and educationally backward' is open to challenge in a Court of law. The Court can acknowledge whether the classification by the Government is arbitrary or is based on any intelligible and tenable principle."

In *Sakal Newspapers Private Ltd v. Union of India*[121], a newspaper publishing private company, two readers and their shareholders, filed a petition against the State. In April 1985, the publishing company filed a lawsuit challenging the provision of the Newspaper (Price and Page) Act, 1956 enabling the government to impose price limits on newspapers as unconstitutional. The petitioners claimed that rights of expression and speech provided under Article 19(1) were violated by the Newspaper Act.

---

119 AIR 1959 SC 149, 183.

120 AIR 1960 Mys 338 at para 23.

121 AIR 1962 SC 305.

Whilst not directly guaranteeing freedom of the press, the Constitution of India has recognized in Article 19(1)(a) as part of freedom of speech that might be limited on the grounds specified in Article 19(2). The right to dissent requires the right to print, discuss and disseminate ideas. The court observed that the order and the Newspaper Act in effect, were to force the newspaper to either increase their rates or decrease the pages by supplying the number of pages maximal for the specific price charging. While the former restricted the distribution of the news on the paper and opinions, the latter would have decreased its circulation substantially. It was a direct violation of the right of journalists in compliance with Article 19(1)(a). An integral aspect of freedom of expression is the newspaper's freedom to publish as well as to circulate any number that they want. The court held newspaper law and the order unconstitutional. The Court however, did not, in light of this relief, consider that the readers too had been infringed on their rights in compliance with Article 19 (1)(a).

Supreme Court of India in *M.R. Balaji v. State of Mysore*[122] declared that the government order to institute categorisation of "backward classes" and "more backward classes" is unlawful & not justified under Article 15(4).

During the Nehruvian era, the first instance of judicial activism on the right to freedom was the case of *Kharak Singh v. the State of UP*[123]. In *Kharak Singh*, a petition was filed under Article 32 of the Constitution in which the petitioner challenged constitutional validity of Chapter XX of U.P. Police Regulations in which Regulation 236 authorized domiciliary visits which breaches the citizens' rights provided under Article19(1)(d) and Article 21 of the Indian Constitution. Here, the police constable would reach his house and yell at his door to awaken him up in the process, based on the grounds of the allegations brought against him. They had put restrictions on him for leaving the town and required him to come to the station on many occasions. The Court ruled that "personal liberty" was not just a person's bodily belief. It means more than just animal life. This applies to life's every shortcoming as

122 AIR 1963 SC 649.
123 AIR 1963 SC 1295

well as abilities. Most judges (via J.C. Shah JJ and K. Subba Rao) hold that personal liberty is a fine word that includes all the varied rights of a man rather than the one mentioned in Article 19.[124]

When they read and considered the relation between Article 19 and 21, the judges broke through by mentioning that:

"If a person's fundamental right under Article 21 is infringed the State can trust upon a law to sustain the action; but that cannot be a complete answer unless said law satisfy the test laid down in Article 19(2) so far as the attributes covered by Article 19(1) are concerned".

This means that State must demonstrate that the constitutional rights are not abused by proving that the legislation endures and that it constitutes a decent limitation within the scope of Article 19(2). But no such protection is required in this petition, because no such statute exists, admittedly. In *Kharak Singh's* case, the petitioner could constitutionally contend that both Article 19(1)(d) and Article 21 guaranteeing his fundamental rights were violated by the actions of the State. Therefore, Kharak Singh was entitled, for this cause, a direction to the respondent – State of Uttar Pradesh, not to resume alleged visits to his home.

Although the courts took on the literal interpreter's position, the Nehruvian period saw, in India, the primitive process of judicial activism.

As stated by Prof S.P. Sathe:

"The Supreme Court of India started as a technocratic court in the 1950s but gradually started acquiring more power through Constitutional interpretation. Its transformation into an activist court has been gradual and imperceptible. The roots of judicial review are to be seen in the court's early assertion regarding the nature of judicial review"[125]

The Parliament kept the baton for the entirety of the Nehru era, and the Court merely replied.

124 Id. at paras 14, 18.

125 Sathe, supra note 21.

POST–NEHRU ERA (1964 – 1974)

The Parliament passed Constitution (Seventeenth Amendment) Act during Nehru's era. This appeal to Parliament's constituent authority was revived after Nehru's death (27 May 1964).

The case of Sajjan Singh v. State of Rajasthan challenged the seventeenth amendment to the Constitution, which added many clauses to 'Ninth Schedule', that prohibited them from violating fundamental rights. Out of five judges that constituted the bench, three judges (Dayal JJ, Wanchoo, and Gajendragadkar C.J.) were completely in agreement with the case of Shankari Prasad. Speaking on behalf of the majority, Chief Justice Gajendragadkar claimed that the constitutional amending power also contained the authority to abolish fundamental rights under Part III. The clauses of paragraph 2 of Article 13(1) were not included by the government in the constitutional amendment and the judicial review of the constitutional amendment is therefore not permissible. However, there were momentous concerns regarding the minority opinion of two judges (M. Hidayatullah and J.R. Mudholkar JJ.). They voiced grave reservations in their distinct but concurrent opinions that fundamental rights should not restrict the amending authority. Justice Hidayatullah said if our basic rights were to be genuinely fundamental, they would not become a "special majority's plaything."

However, the optimism that regulated previous legislations was thin in later years, particularly during the Nehru period. The Parliament had sufficient authority to implement the land revolution, which, however, did not occur. Instead, the green movement happened, and the grip of the great owners only tightened. As the result, the Constitution (Forty-Fourth Amendment) Act of 1978 omitted the rights from the chapter on fundamental rights.[126]

126 Constitution (Forty-fourth Amendment) Act, 1978, Section 6, Acts of Parliament, 1978.

In the case of P. Vajravelu Mudaliar v. Special Deputy Collector,[127] Madras, Supreme Court accepted that it is not justifiable to get inflate the claims in pre-defined cases but clarified that the overall amount of compensatory goods would equal the value of the property in question. The pay-out should be substantial.

Here, the I.C. Golak Nath and others v. State of Punjab and Anr[128], which was judged by an eleven judges bench of the Supreme Court, where from Sajjan Singh and Sankari Prasad, the disagreement ratio stood 6:5. They observed that constitutional rights were not open to amendment & that the power of amendment over Part III as conceded by the Sankari Prasad & Sajjan Singh cases, that was based on Article 13(2) and Article 368 is an erroneous view. Therefore, the decision was not retrospective, however it did not invalidate the constitution amendment controversy raised in the court. Three writ petitions were moved in the Golak Nath case. One of these was Golak Nath's mother, daughter, and grandsons. The inclusion of the Punjab Protection of Land Tenures Act of 1953 in the Ninth Schedule, which was contained in the 1st, 4th and the 7th Amendment, allegedly abridged fundamental rights, and was prayed through this petition to be declared unconstitutional. The "Mysore Land Reforms Act" was also attacked on the same grounds in the other two petitions.[129] Already in Sajjan Singh and Sankari Prasad cases, the Supreme Court in the judgments had granted much of the claims presented in aid of the respondents as well as the petitioners as described.

It cannot be agreed more that authority for amending constitution shall be a power of the sovereign, which are superior to legislative power, unwarranted by tacit limits, and with which the changes made to that power also include political issues that are outside the control of judicial scrutiny. It is important not to object at the concept of sovereign power, since its sovereignty is only within a given constitutional boundary. When articles are expressed in disagreement as broadly as possible, the Court shall be allowed to constrict and harmonize them. There

127 AIR 1965 SC 1017.

128 AIR 1967 SC 1643: (1967) 2 SCR 762"

129 Id. at 1669, 1718

is nothing in the essence of the amending authority that requires this House to resolve any express or implicit limits on that power.[130]

The case of *Golak Nath* started the great war of judicial versus parliamentary supremacy, which was quite distinct from the earlier skirmished war. Issues related to property and other crucial units of the constitution which ran through Indian politics and would continue to run, were resurrected and revived over decades.

In the judicial and legal fraternity, *Golak Nath's* decision often met with great concern. 'What has given Court the privilege not to change the Constitution?' The duty of the Court was to state and not to tell what the Constitution offers. Eminent lawyers and academicians at that time shared a 'strong' reply. It was just a few days after the Golak Nath case decision as well as his entry into politics, which triggered a huge flutter, that Chief Justice Subba Rao resigned for contesting election for the President's office with all the support of opposition political parties.

The Supreme Court's rulings in two cases – a. The *H. H. Madhav Rao Scindia v. Union of India* ('*Privy Purses*' case)"[131] and b. *The Rustom Cavasjee Cooper v. Union of India*[132] (Bank Nationalization case) once again opened the conflicting topic of rights related to property.

In Indira Gandhi's agenda for supremacy and power was the nationalization of banks as well as the abolition of private purses of the former princely state rulers, which were considered to be populist measures.[133]

During the post-Nehruvian era, the advocacy for bank nationalization grew more strongly. The plea was based on Article 39 of the Directive Principles of the State Policy, which provides for distribution of the common goods or management of the state's

---

130 I.C. Golak Nath v. State of Punjab, AIR 1967 SC 1643, 1658, 1659, 1669, 1707: (1967) 2 SCR 762.

131 AIR 1971 SC 530

132 AIR 1970 SC 564

133 Granville Austin, Working A Democratic Constitution – A History of The Indian Experience 209 (Oxford University Press, New Delhi, Eight Impression, 2011).

material resources to subserve the common goal and assures that the economic architecture does not contribute to the accumulation of wealth and ultimately means for production of common goods. The nationalization of banks preceded the 1954 resolution of the Congress Party on the "socialist pattern" and on 19 July 1968, the order declaring the nationalization of banks was passed.

The order was subsequently challenged by Sir Rustom Cavasjee Cooper and other members of civil society by filing a petition against the powers of the President while claiming their rights under Articles 14, 19 as well as 31. Despite Attorney General Niren De's claim that nationalization was a government action and hence could not be challenged before the courts, the High Court's seven-judges bench suspended the government & gave the nationalized banks orders under the 1968's Banking Companies Act.[134] Even though the order of the Supreme Court was expanded, the Parliament passed the Nationalization Bill instead.

On 10 February 1970, before the eleven judges' bench of the Supreme Court comprising of I.D. Dua, P. Jaganmohan Reddy, A.N. Ray, A.N. Grover, K.S. Hegde, C.A. Vaidialingam, G.K. Mitter, V. Bhargava, J.M. Shelat, S.M. Sikri, and J.C. Shah, JJ.), the constitutionality of the Bank Nationalization Act was challenged. Rustom Cavasjee Cooper, the chief claimant, argued that the Act breached its basic equal rights according to Article 14 and that the land reimbursement taken was insufficient under Article 31 and Article 19(1)(f).

Justice J.C. Shah, in the judgment (ten out of eleven judges formed the majority view), ruled the Act to be declared unconstitutional. He observed that Court was unable to decide whether or not the extent of compensation was appropriate, however, the compensation concept defined in a law for the collection of property did not go outside the inspection of judicial authority.[135] On the other end, Justice A.N. Ray, who differed from majority view, held that, on grounds with which the compensations were payable and those standards were just or not, cannot be challenged in the Court. In this respect, Justice A.N. Ray

134 Id. at pg 215

135 AIR 1970 SC 564, at para 90."

further noted that criteria for deciding if the values are all applicable for compensation or whether compensation is illustrative and cannot be that of "just equivalent." If the fixed number is not evident and outrageously illusory or if the rules are relevant to set off, Article 13(2) shall not be broken.[136]

Therefore, the case of *Rustom Cavasjee Cooper* was a post-Nehruvian militant decision in which the Court objected the Executive's political decision and held in favour of right to fair compensation in cases of acquisition of property being compulsorily acquired.

The Constitution (Twenty-fifth Amendment) Act, 1971 which deleted the term "compensation" and replaced it with more undesirable terms, such as "amount," was passed. The Court, although, tended to take opinion that term 'sum' still implied that the worth of the land obtained by the State was returned fairly.

The historic case of the *Kesavananda Bharati v. the State of Kerala*[137] is the case of the basic structure doctrine. In that case, the constitutional validity of the Kerala Land Reforms Act, 1963 (revised in 1969), had initially been questioned.

However, when the twenty-ninth Amendment placed the petitioner's case under the Ninth Schedule of the Constitution, the petitioner questioned the validity of the twenty-fifth, twenty-sixth, and twenty-ninth Constitutional amendments as well. A bench of thirteen Judges of Supreme Court heard the petition. For a Parliament to be allowed to exert its full legislative authority to destroy or remove Constitution's fundamental provisions, basic elements, and essential features, the petitioner argued that this construction is to be declared unconstitutional for the following reasons:

1. With the only constituent right bestowed on it by the Constitution, provided to it by the citizens, the Parliament cannot expand its authority to annul the restriction on the terms conferred on its power to amend.

136 Id. at para 201, 204

137 AIR 1973 SC 1461, (1973) 4 SSC 225.

2. Parliament cannot provide itself the right to change, alter or replace all of the basic features of the Constitution unless it has become a functionary under the Constitution.

3. To allow Parliament itself to strip away or ignore any, of the constitutional rights, the fundamental human rights & liberty which the people have reserved for themselves in compliance with the Constitution, cannot continue.

4. Parliament does not at first have the ability to modify or destroy the basic structure of the Constitution but must acknowledge inferred, fundamental limitations of the amending process. Therefore, Parliament cannot eliminate the limits on its constitutional power by eliminating those restrictions or pretending to have the power for altering or destroying some of these fundamental laws.

Mutually the Judges were of the opinion that the Constitution (Twenty-fourth Amendment) Act is relevant and that as per the amendment the Parliament has the ability to change any part, even those on human rights, or any of the clauses of the Constitution. Subsequently, seven Judges (Mukherjee, Khanna, Jaganmohan Reddy, Grover, Hedge, Shelat, C.J. and Sikri, JJ) held that there are certain tacit and intrinsic limits to the power of amendment provided under Article 368 and that Parliament should not modify the Constitution's basic structure in the exercise of this power. Six of these (except Khanna, J.) considered that the essential framework or the meaning of the Constitution is related to the constitutional rights set out in Part III of the Constitution, and thus cannot be modified.

However, the six judges (Chandrachud, Dwivedi, Beg, Mathew, Palekar, and Ray, JJ.) were not able to consider a constraint on the legislative authority to amend the Constitution. However, Khanna, J. apprehended the laws related to property were not a fundamental part of the framework in the constitutional sense, and titled the equilibrium in majority creation with Chandrachud, Dwivedi, Beg, Mathew, Palekar and Ray, JJ.

The concept of basic structure was described by Chief Justice Sikri, through providing illustrations, like:

- Constitutional supremacy
- The democratic and republican form of the Government
- The secular character of the Constitution
- Separation of powers among the judiciary, the executive as well as the legislature
- The federal character of the Constitution

He has indicated that structure is developed on the fundamental foundations, which are closely related to an individual's freedom as well as dignity and that cannot be destroyed by any form of an amendment.[138]

The fundamental elements of Constitutional structure that were already specified by Chief Justice Sikri, were illustrated by Shelat and Grover, JJ.

- The mandate for building a welfare State included in Part IV of the Constitution
- Integrity and unity of the Nation.[139]
- In the same manner, Mukherjee and Hede, JJ. outlined the Constitution's fundamental features or basic elements for example:
- Indian sovereignty
- Our polity's democratic character
- The country's unity
- Fundamental characteristics of an individual's freedom to be protected for the citizens

138 Id. at 366 (paras 292-293).
139 Id. at 454 (para 582).

– The mandate for building an egalitarian society and welfare state.[140]

The elements of the basic structure were discovered by Jaganmohan Reddy, which was similar to the elements specified in its preamble as well as explained in several provisions.

According to the 'summary' signed by nine out of thirteen judges in *Kesavananda Bharati*, the majority, in that case, overruled *Golak Nath* and held that Article 368 did not enable Parliament to change the basic structure or framework of the constitution. The majority also invalidated the second part of Article 31C, introduced by the twenty-fifth Amendment, which excluded the jurisdiction of the courts to enquire whether a law protected under that article gave effect to the policy of securing the Directive Principles, viz the directives in Article 39(b), and (c).

When the Kesavananda Bharati was being decided, the Congress Party led by Mrs. Indira Gandhi, had an overwhelming majority in the new parliament.[141] The ruling party interpreted Kesavananda Bharati as a coup by the judges to gain supremacy from the Parliament. The government, therefore, retaliated decisively. Its first strategy was to dissolve the Kesavananda Bharati majority.[142]

Chief Justice Sikri was about to retire within a few days from day the verdict in *Kesavananda Bharati* was rendered. Till that time, the practice had been to appoint the senior-most judge of the Supreme Court as the Chief Justice. If that rule were to be followed, Justice Shelat must have been appointed as Chief Justice. However, he would have had a very brief tenure & would have been succeeded by Justice Hegde. But the government stunned everybody by appointing Justice A. N. Ray as Chief Justice in preference to three judges, namely Grover, Hegde, and Shelat who were senior to him. These three judges resigned in protest. The *Kesavananda* majority was therefore reduced by four judges. Justice Mukherjee died & Justice Reddy was to retire soon.

140 Id. at 637-638 (para 1159)."
141 Sathe, *supra* note 21
142 *Ibid.*

Out of the seven judges who subscribed to the doctrine of the basic structure doctrine, only Justice Khanna remained.

As stated by Fali S. Nariman:

"To critics of Golak Nath, I would only say that if there was no Golak Nath, there would have been no Kesavananda Bharati – and if the unchecked powers of the amendment were not acknowledged, we would have walked the way as some of our neighbours; since ruling party continuously had a massive majority; we would have almost definitely institutionalized a dictatorship through a Constitutional amendment: by amending the Constitution to provide for a 'presidential form of government': a euphemism used in this part of the world for autocratic rule. And with a dictatorship, we would have lost the freedom of the Press & the independence of the Judiciary."[143]

EMERGENCY ERA (1975-1977)

The judgment in *Indira Gandhi v Raj Narain*[144] was delivered during the period of emergency and it was applauded as being the finest hour in the lifetime of the Supreme Court.[145] An event that indirectly precipitated the declaration of emergency in 1975 was the verdict of the High Court of Allahabad by which Mrs. Indira Gandhi's election to the Lok Sabha was set aside on the ground that she resorted to a corrupt practices as defined in the Representation of the People's Act, 1951, known as the *Election Law*. Her opponents put pressure on her to resign. She had challenged the judgment of the High Court of Allahabad before the Supreme Court, and the Supreme Court had admitted her appeal, subsequently staying the execution of the High Court's decree. There was already a proclamation of emergency in operation, which had been made in 1971 when India fought a war with Pakistan for liberation of Bangladesh. While the previous proclamation was intended to counter the danger of external aggression, the 1975

143 Fali S. Nariman, The Judiciary & the Role of the Pathfinders, Lokendra Malik (Ed.), Judicial Activism In India 43 (Universal Law Publishing Co. pvt. Ltd, New Delhi, 2014)."

144 AIR 1975 SC 1590.

145 H. M. Seervai, The Emergency, Future Safeguards & The Habeas Corpus Case 4 (N M Tripathi Pvt Ltd, Bombay, 1978).

emergency was for controlling the situation created by the threat of internal disturbance. Several members of Parliament belonging to the opposition were arrested. During that time, Parliament passed several constitutional amendments.[146]

The Thirty-ninth Amendment specified that any controversy involving the election to Parliament of the persons holding office of the Prime Minister & the Speaker shall be referred to a body to be appointed by the Parliament and this was to apply even to those cases that has been pending or being decided by the courts in conformity with the statute as it existed before this amendment came into force. Article 329-A clause (4) inserted by the Thirty-ninth amendment stated that:

"No law made by Parliament before the commencement of the Constitution (Thirty-Ninth Amendment) Act, 1975, in so far as it relates to election petitions and matters connected therewith, shall apply or shall be deemed ever to have applied to or concerning the election of any person who was holding office of the Prime Minister or the Speaker to either house of Parliament & such election shall not be deemed to be void or ever to have become void on any ground on which such election could be declared to be void or had before the commencement of the amendment been declared to be void under any law."

Furthermore, it has been stated that:

"Notwithstanding any order made by any court before such commencement, declaring such election to be void, such election shall continue to be valid in all respects & any such order & any finding on which such order is based shall be deemed always to have been void and of no effect."

The amendments were passed with a view to prevent scrutiny of Mrs. Gandhi's election to the Lok Sabha by the court. It was introduced in the Lok Sabha on August 7 and passed in that house on the same day; the Rajya Sabha passed it on August 8, and it was ratified by half the legislature of the States on August 9 and obtained the President's

146 S.P. Sathe, Constitutional Amendments 1950-1988: Law and Politics (N M Tripathi Pvt Ltd, Bombay, 1989)."

assent on August 10. Indira Gandhi's appeal was scheduled to be taken before the Supreme Court on 11 August.[147]

When Mrs. Gandhi's appeal came up for hearing, the learned Attorney General presented that in view of the Thirty-Ninth Amendment, the Court had nothing to hear because the original decision itself had been wiped out. In reply to that, Mr. Shanti Bhushan appearing for the respondent challenged the validity of the said Amendment itself on the ground that it destroyed the basic structure of the Constitution.

The *Prime Minister Election case* was heard by a bench of five judges. They were Justices Chandrachud, Mathew, Beg, Khanna, and Chief Justice Ray. All except Justice Khanna had held in *Kesavananda Bharati* that there were no limitations upon the power of constitutional amendments. Justice Khanna had agreed to the basic structure doctrine. Chief Justice Ray and Justice Mathew did not uphold the impugned amendment because in their opinion the constituent power could not be employed to exercise judicial power. Justice Beg used the conventional technique of the English law to frustrate the ouster clauses, which did not exclude a judicial review on appeal of the Allahabad judgment. However, Justices Chandrachud, Khanna, and Mathew on the grounds of its compatibility with the basic structure of the Constitution, held the impugned amendment invalid.

Although Court unanimously ruled that the challenged amendment was null and invalid, only three judges were unmistakably conscious that it breached the Constitution's underlying framework. Therefore, they preferred the third alternative to uphold the election but striking down the impugned amendment. This allowed the Court to assert its power of judicial review over the constituent power of the Parliament while avoiding direct conflict by political entity. The ruling establishment was satisfied that, by dismissing Raj Narain's appeal on merits, the Court gave legal validity to the election of Mrs. Gandhi. Saving her election through the protection offered by the Thirty-Ninth Amendment would have been a lesser pleasure than getting it held valid

147 H. M. Seervai, Constitutional Law of India 1519 (N.M. Tripathi Pvt Ltd, Bombay, 2nd edn., 1976).

by the Court on the merit. Because of the euphoria generated by the decision holding the election valid on merit, the ruling class connived at the unfavourable part of that verdict, which upheld its right to revisit constitutional amendments. The Court reclaimed this power.

The *Prime Minister Election Case* provided social validity to the basic structure doctrine. When that doctrine was laid down in *Kesavananda Bharati*, it was judged in the context of the Court–Parliament competition for finality that had been going on since *Golak Nath*. But the *Prime Minister Election* introduced it in an entirely different context. The Thirty-ninth Amendment was suggestive of the withdrawn bill of attainder, which was known in English constitutional literature. A bill of attainder was a way to prosecute an individual using the legislative process & was viewed as a high watermark of autocratic arbitrariness. People who felt that the unlimited power to Parliament to amend the Constitution might be abused was an argument of fear that had been before them; concrete evidence of how majoritarian partisanship could cause the total demise of the rule of law. This also lent credibility to the underlying institutional constraint on the constituent power of the parliament.[148]

Professor Upendra Baxi has significantly examined these decisions in his book 'The Indian Supreme Court and Politics'. As stated by him the Court had three options:

1. It could have upheld the amendment but after investigating the validity of election on merits.
2. It could have struck down the amendment as well as also considered Mrs. Gandhi's election to be void, or
3. It could have struck down the amendment without getting through the election's merits and thereby uphold Ms. Gandhi's election.

The first choice would have cost the court its reputation. Their social confidence might have diminished. The second choice might

148 S.P. Sathe, Limitations on Constitutional Amendment: Basic Structure Principle Re-examined, Rajeev Dhavan & Alice Jacob (eds), Indian Constitution: Trends and Issues 179 (N M Tripathi, 1978).

have led to the Court itself being destabilized, as the Executive had power to appoint the judges. The executive had already suspended three top-ranking judges who in *Kesavananda Bharati* had decided against the government. Perhaps the self-preserving impulses convinced the judges not to take that path.[149]

ATTEMPT TO REVERSE THE BASIC STRUCTURE DOCTRINE

Indira Nehru Gandhi v. Raj Narain provided the Supreme Court a chance to re-examine the doctrine of basic structure as applied in the case of *Kesavannanda Bharati*. The government sought to reverse the decision of *Kesavananda* while matter was still pending. The Attorney General and Tamil Nadu's Advocate General moved an application before Chief Justice Ray that several writ petitions be listed for hearing on 10 November 1975 to reconsider the basic structure doctrine. Following *Kesavananda Bharti*, it was argued that the amendment affected free & fair elections and judicial review, and these being part of the basic structure of the constitution was unconstitutional. Besides, it was argued that Parliament in the exercise of the constituent power was not competent to exercise power to validate an election that is declared void by the High Court.

Chief Justice Ray was persuaded to set up a thirteen judges' special bench for reconsidering *Kesavananda Bharati's* majority judgment. The new bench comprised of Justices Untwalia, Fazl Ali, Singhal, Gupta, Goswami, Sarkaria, Krishna Iyer, Bhagwati, Chandrachud, Mathew, Beg, and Khanna, and Ray himself. Khanna alone had dedicated himself to the basic structure doctrine. Others were not committed.

Justice Khanna, whose judgment in the *Fundamental Rights case* was decisive in tilting the scale in favour of the basic structure doctrine, took this opportunity to clarify his position on the order fundamental rights vis-à-vis the right to property, as discussed earlier. He said that he had clearly hinted in his judgment in *Kesavananda* that fundamental rights were part of basic structure. This clarification made his judgment in *Kesavananda* utterly preposterous and self-contradictory as he had

149 Upendra Baxi, The Indian Supreme Court & Politics 46 (Eastern Book Company, Lucknow, 1980).

upheld two constitutional amendments concerning fundamental rights. So Chief Justice might have hoped that it would not be difficult to get at least seven judges to vote against the basic structure doctrine.

However, before the hearing could take place on 10 November, a constitution bench of five judges, comprising Chief Justice A.N. Ray and Justices Khanna, Beg, Mathew and Chandrachud, heard the Election case & pronounced its judgment on 7 November itself.

The court upheld Mrs. Gandhi's election but struck down the amendment as violative of the basic feature of the Constitution. On 10 November 1975, the hearing began on the reconsideration of the basic structure doctrine. But when the Court asks Attorney General to establish prima facie that the basic structure limitation on Parliament's power of Constitutional amendment would come in the way of social progress, no satisfactory evidence of such an eventuality was produced and, ultimately, on 12 November the special bench had to be dissolved.

The basic structure doctrine is the high watermark of judicial activism. The Supreme Court of India only enjoys such power. It has also been claimed by the Supreme Court of Bangladesh. Such power imposes an onerous burden on the Court. The Court must allow legitimate changes to the Constitution but, at the same time ensure prevention of erosion of all values that constitute very soul of Constitutionalism.

Justice Jackson is often quoted,

"Court is not final because it is infallible, but it is infallible because it is final."

The people live with the Court's infallibility if they believe that erroneous decisions can be corrected and that even its errors are not due to its lack of impartiality or lack of objectivity. There is therefore even greater need to examine to whom the Supreme Court is accountable and how such accountability is reinforced.[150]

For a long time, the court had such a positivist stance, another example of it being its decision during the 1975 emergency in *A.D.M.*

150 Seervai, *supra* note 149 at 99

Jabalpur v. Shiv Kant Shukla[151]. During the Emergency, leaders of the opposition were put in prison, the press was muzzled & fundamental rights suspended. This case arose out of the appeals filed by the States against the decisions of different High Courts taking a liberal approach and allowing habeas corpus petitions filed by the detainees on grounds of non-compliance with law or *mala fides.* A preliminary objection had been raised by the Union of India and/or the States that in view of the Presidential Order dated 27 June 1975 under Article 359, which suspended the right of any person to approach any court for enforcement of his fundamental rights under the Articles 14, 19, 21 and 22, the petitioners had no *locus standi* to maintain the petition. The reason being in substance, they were seeking to enforce their fundamental right granted by the Article 21. The High Courts of Allahabad, Bombay, Delhi, Karnataka, Madhya Pradesh, Punjab, Rajasthan did not find much force in the preliminary objection of the Union of States and ruled that though the petitioners could not move the court to enforce their fundamental right by the Article 21, as they were required to show that the order of detention was not under or in compliance with the relevant law or was *mala fide.* In appeal, the Supreme Court turned down the stand of the seven High Courts and legitimized the intrusion by the State of the personal liberty of the people.

In this case, the Court held by the majority of four that during the proclamation of emergency under Article 352 of the Constitution, a court was powerless to protect an individual from the action of the State even if such an action was contrary to the law and resulted in total negation of his/her right to life or liberty. Even Seervai, who had approved of the Court's positivism in *Gopalan*,[152] was vociferous in condemning the Court's self-abnegation in *Shukla.*[153]

Justice Chandrachud, as he then was, while responding to the argument that unless a presidential order was read down, it might give power to the government to arbitrarily shoot down any person, said:

151 AIR 1976 SC 1207
152 AIR 1950 SC 27.
153 AIR 1976 SC 1207.

"Counsel later expressed the fear that during an emergency, the executive may whip and strip and starve the detainee and if this is our judgment, even shoot him down. Such misdeeds haven't tarnished the record of Free India and I have a diamond-bright, diamond-hard hope that such things will never come to pass."[154]

Justice Beg, as he then was, went even ahead of Justice Chandrachud in giving a clean chit to the emergency regime and infamously remarked in his judgment in praise of the Government. He said:

"Further, we understand the care along concern bestowed by the State authorities upon the welfare of the detainees who are well-housed, well-fed and well-treated, is almost maternal."[155]

The lone dissenter in this case, Justice Khanna paid a heavy price for his disagreement. He was superseded to the post of Chief Justice of India by Justice Beg for a court that had always stood up for individual rights and liberty, the ruling left a lasting scar.

The Supreme Court's power of review, as means of legitimizing the government's action, was once again exercised in *State of Rajasthan v. Union of India*[156]. In this case, the constitutionality of the letter issued by the Union Home Minister, Charan Singh was challenged under Article 131 of the Constitution. The impugned letter was issued to the Chief Ministers of nine States (where the Congress party had suffered a setback in the parliamentary election) urging them to advise their respective Governors to dissolve the State Assemblies in view of the unprecedented defeat of the parliamentary elections.

POST EMERGENCY ERA (1978 ONWARDS)

The post-emergency era witnessed an increasing trend, of the courts exercising their powers for the greater cause: in matters ranging from custodial deaths, abolition of bonded labour, regulating pollution, etc., further enlarging the scope of 'Right to Life'. The judiciary time & again called upon the executive to perform its obligations under the law. The Supreme Court on various occasions also highlighted

154 AIR 1976 SC 1207, 1349.
155 Id. at 1319.
156 "(1977) 3 SCC 592: AIR 1977 SC 1361.

the need of judicial restraint for the maintenance of the balance of power of different pillars in the democratic system of the country. In a democracy like India, the Constitution is supreme, and the rule of law demands that each organ of the state sticks to the constitutional mandate.

Numerous Public Interest Litigation matters in this period substantially enriched environmental jurisprudence. The Supreme Court, in the *Oleum gas leak* case, propounded the doctrine of absolute liability and gave directions that expanded the scope of Article 32 of the Constitution of India.

However, the post-emergency era and the ambit of all that happened there is so enormous, that it requires a separate and elaborate description. Therefore, the era of 'Post Emergency Judicial Activism' has been later dealt with in the book.

FINDINGS

Thus, we can conclude that during the Nehru years, the Court did not cross swords with the executive but on the contrary legitimized State intervention for controlling the economy and enacting social justice, barring a few cases on right to property. On matters such as freedom of speech and protective discrimination, it legislated interstitially. On personal liberty, it adopted various techniques of administrative law to protect the liberty of the individual. Whenever Court thought that the Executive should not be embarrassed, particularly where questions of national security were involved, it stepped carefully.[157]

In those days, judicial activism as favoured state intervention was welcomed. It is notable that, ever since the late 1950s, the court began to perceive that it had a larger role to play in umpiring Indian democracy. But even in these cases, the Court felt bounded by the limitations of the text of the Constitution. Whenever it got an opportunity to fill in the interstices, it did. But it did not overtly claim that it had the authority to give a construction that would challenge the positivist approach to constitutional interpretation.[158]

157 May, *supra* note 67 at 61
158 *Ibid.*

Between 1950 and 1967 the country witnessed an agrarian revolution through the several land reform legislations that were passed within this period. All these land welfare legislations were upheld by the Court in *Shankari Prasad Singh Deo's* case and *Sajjan Singh's* case on the ground that to implement the land reforms policy, the Parliament had the power to amend the fundamental rights and such amendments were out of the judicial scrutiny even if they infringed the said rights.

At the same time Court was aware that if the Parliament had the ultimate power to take away fundamental rights without any exception, a time might come when we would indiscernibly and eventually enter a totalitarian rule.[159] By 1966, parliament passed as many as twenty amendments to the Constitution.

In *Golak Nath's* case, Chief Justice Hidayatullah stated that:

"In our Country, amendments so far had been made only with the object of negativing Supreme Court's decisions."[160]

The liability to pay compensation was reiterated in *R.C. Cooper v. India*[161]. Today we see that the right to property is being asserted not by the rich but by the poor. Now it is being asserted by those who are the evicted from their lands by the State in order to bring about development. The Supreme Court struggled to keep itself alive and sustain people's faith in *Indira Gandhi v. Raj Narain*[162]

But what it managed to save here, it lost in *A.D.M. Jabalpur v. Shiv Kant Shukla.*[163]

---

159 Justice V.G. Palshikar, Judicial Activism, 8 AIR J 201-205 (1998).
160 AIR 1967 SC 1643.
161 AIR 1970 SC 564.
162 AIR 1975 SC 2299.
163 AIR 1976 SC 1207.

6. HORIZONS OF JUDICIAL ACTIVISM

"Power tends to corrupt, and absolute power corrupts absolutely"

The above-mentioned quote was by John Emerich Edward Dalberg Acton, first Baron Acton (1834–1902). The historian and moralist, who were otherwise known as Lord Acton, expressed this opinion in a letter to Bishop Mandell Creighton in 1887. The context of the phrase supports the doctrine of separation of power. The goal of our Constitution, enunciated by our worthy founding fathers, in its preamble is to secure a 'welfare state.' For achieving this goal, the Constitution has created three organs - the Legislature, the Executive, and the Judiciary.[164]

An insipid justification for judicial activism is that courts should ensure that justice is done. In this process, the boundaries between the Legislature, the Executive, and the Judiciary are breached leading to the violation of the doctrine of separation of powers. The question is how to ensure justice. The Roman sentential '*fiat justicia ruat coelum*' caused some misconception as it is translated to mean *let justice prevail even though heavens may fall.* There is an opinion that the translation of '*justicia*' into modern *justice* is a mistranslation. In fact, for the Romans, justice meant their system of law, '*fiat jus ruat justiciam*' translated as *let the law prevail though justice may fall.*

This doctrine can be carried to the extreme, as was done by a Maltese judge. Malta is a small island that didn't have room for more than one judge. In the eighteenth century, there was a judge named Cambro. One early morning while he was looking out of the window, he saw a man running and another frantically chasing him.

Ultimately, the victim was overtaken just under his window and brutally stabbed with a knife. Just then the assailant saw a constable at some distance and fled, leaving the knife in the wound and the sheath behind. Soon afterward a baker happened to pass by with his basket

---

164 Justice B.P. Jeeven Reddy, Judicial Activism: A Perspective, The Hindu (Delhi) April 30, 2008

of bread, found the victim lying dead. As he tried to take the knife out of the wound, he saw a constable coming towards him from a distance and was utterly terrified. He took the blood-stained sheath of the knife in his hand, put it into his basket, and hid himself somewhere near the entrance of a neighbouring house. Judge Cambro saw all this with his own eyes.

The constable arrived there found the dead body warm and still bleeding. He surmised that the murderer must be hiding somewhere close. He searched soon found the baker with his hand stained with blood & the sheath in his basket fitted with the knife.

Frightened, he lost his wit and gave incoherent replies during interrogation. The baker was put on trial before judge Cambro. Since no other judge was present, he had to try him. He found that circumstantial evidence against the baker was clinching enough to convict him: he was found hiding near to the place of occurrence immediately after the murder, his hands was stained with blood & weapon used for the crime was found in his possession. Despite knowing personally that he was innocent, the judge pronounced him guilty of murder as required by the law, sentenced him to death, and the baker was executed.

Later when to the truth surfaced and the real story came to be known, a horrified public demanded Cambro's blood, but some jurists supported and lauded his decision. He had done justice according to law not withstanding his knowledge that baker was innocent. On similar evidence, he would have convicted anyone, and so he did with the baker.[165]

A confrontation between different wings of government is not the result of clarity or ambiguity. It is a function of the struggle for power, and every wing tramples on others when it is strong. Antonio Gramsci aptly described this:

"The separation of powers...is a product of the struggle among civil society, political society in a specific historical period. In other words, there takes place within the society what Croce calls the 'perpetual conflict between Church and State' in which the Church is taken as representing the totality of civil

165 Thomas Dunphy & Thomas J. Cummins, Remarkable Trials of All Countries 453 (Ward & Peloubер, New York, 1978).

society (whereas in fact, it is only an element of diminishing importance within it) and the State as representing every attempt to crystallize permanently a particular stage of development, a particular situation. In this sense, the Church itself might become State, and the conflict may occur between, the secular (and secularizing) civil society, and on the other State/Church. Unity of the State in the differentiation of powers can be understood as the Parliament to be more closely linked to civil society, where the Judicial supervision, between government and Parliament, represents the continuity of the written law (even against the government). Naturally, all three powers are also organs of political hegemony, but in different degrees: 1. Legislature; 2. Judiciary; 3. Executive. It is also to be noted that lapses in the administration of justice make a disastrous impression on the public: the hegemonic apparatus is more sensitive in the sector, to which arbitrary actions on the part of the police & polity may also be referred."[166]

166 Antonio Gramsci, Selections against the Prison Notebooks 245-246 (Orient Longman, Hyderabad, 1998).

7. ORIGIN OF SEPARATION OF POWER

Aristotle believed that there would be a small unit in charge of good governance. The political enlightenment French thinker, Charles-Louis de Secondat, better known as Baron de Montesquieu in his *Spirit of Laws*[167]. propounded the doctrine of the separation powers to maintain checks and balance. He coined the term 'Separation of powers' which became guiding principles of the constitutions of modern democratic states. The model is also known as *Trias Politica*. Aristotle conceived a mixed government comprising the noblest elements of monarchy, aristocracy, and democracy, rating none as perfect. The ancient Greeks developed it first and incorporated it into the constitutions that governed their city-state, but it only became prevalent during the Roman Republic. Its constitution provided for the separation of powers where the state was divided into branches or estates, each with separate & independent powers and areas of responsibility – the Executive, the Legislature, and the Judiciary.

James Harrington, in his *Oceana*, had refined these concepts to propose structures based on the separation of powers.[168] Montesquieu argued that:

"There is no liberty where judicial power is not separated from both legislative and executive power. If judicial & legislative powers are not separated, power over the life & liberty of citizens would be arbitrary, because the judge would also be a legislator. If it were not separated against executive power, judge will accept the strength of an oppressor."[169]

"Miserable indeed would be the case, where the same man, or the same body, whether of the nobles or of the people, to exercise those three powers,

---

167 Charles De Secondat, Baron De Montesquieu, The Spirit of Laws (Legal Classics Library, Alabama Gryphon Editions Ltd, Special Ed. 1984).

168 James Harrington, The Commonwealth of Oceana 87 (Livewell Chapman, London, 1656)."

169 Secondat, *supra* note 169.

that of enacting laws, that of executing the public resolutions, and that of judging the crimes or differences of individuals."[170]

Thus Montesquieu, the great political philosopher of the Enlightenment, argued in favour of a system of governance in which different branches of government exercise different powers to avoid concentration of powers and preserve human liberty—the Legislature should make law, the Executive should execute it, and the Judiciary should settle disputes under the law. This is the doctrine of separation of powers.

While the proponents of this doctrine claim that it preserves freedom by the avoidance of a tyrannical system, its critics fail to accept it as well as pointing out that representative democracies never succeeded in combining control. Walter Bagehot subscribed and criticized Hobbes' opinion that sovereignty was fragmented. He thought that it was damaging to the health of the nation if at times of crisis one person is not in a position to take a final decision.[171]

It was not until persistent developments compelled the complicating transposition of the *Separation of Powers* theory into one of convenient 'division of function.' The power was consolidated in the hands of the monarch until the advent of democracy in the present form. The monarch's power was absolute and unqualified. His role evolved from the idea of a single person acting as the leader of the community. The history of Rome tells us that the emperors had absolute controls over the empire and its citizens. In Britain, Royal power was limited for first time when King John Lackland was forced to sign an agreement in June 1215 popularly known as the *Magna Carta.* King James I believed in the Divine Rights of Kings and defined his prerogative as absolute. In the struggle between the Executive, the Legislature, and the Judiciary,

170 *Ibid.*

171 Walter Bagehot, Its Supposed Checks and Balances in The English Constitution, 214- 238 (12th Impression, Glasgow: Fontana/Collins, 1976).

it was Chief Justice Edward Coke who, in 1608, displayed his muscles by asserting the power of judicial proclamations whenever he wished.[172]

For the king's supremacy, Bracton in 'Rex non debetesse sub homine sed Deo et lege', an article written in King Henry III time, stated:

"That the king should not be under man, but under God & the law."

Whilst King James I articulated his motivation for deciding cases by himself on the argument that:

"I always thought, and I have heard the boast, that your English Law is founded upon reason. If that be so, why have not I and others reason as well as you the judges?"

To this, Lord Coke CJ responded:

"True it is, please, Your Majesty, that God endowed Your Majesty with excellent science as well as great gifts of nature; but Your Majesty will allow me to say, with all reverence, that you are not learned in the laws of your realm of England... where law is an art that requires long study & experience before a man can attain take cognizance of it. The law is the golden met-wand and measure to try the causes of Your Majesty's subjects, and it is by the law that Your Majesty is protected in safety and peace."[173]

But in 1616, James I dismissed Coke because he declined to make judgments on the king's liking. The history was repeated ten years later when Sir Ranulph Crewe, Chief Justice, was dismissed by Charles I. When James II, the second son of Charles I, ascended the throne in 1685, he dissolved the Parliament. This triggered off a nationwide movement. The struggle with the monarchy & Parliament culminated in the Bill of Rights (1689) from which originated the fundamental rights. The king lost his power to arrest anyone arbitrarily. It was the most important act after *Magna Carta* which trimmed the power of the king. In later centuries, John Locke and James Harrington had advocated the doctrine of separation of powers, when they came together to draft the American Constitution. Montesquieu's' writings had considerably

172 Thomas Bonham v. College of Physicians (Dr Bonham's case), 8 Co. Rep. 107a; 77 Eng. Rep. 638 (C.P. 1610).

173 *Ibid.*

influenced the opinions and thoughts of the constitutional builders. Thomas Jefferson, one of their founding fathers and the third president of the US, was an ardent proponent of the doctrine of separation of powers in the context of governmental functioning. About 60 years before the drafting of the American Constitution, the British in 1688 had, introduced the Bill of Rights, which had as one of its characteristic features: the separation of powers between King & the Parliament; the King & the Common Law courts. The makers of the American Constitution adopted the concept and fitted it into their written Constitution.

This extension has been so dramatic since Industrial Revolution and has since 1900 followed so steadily on the growth of legislative intervention in new areas of economic and social relations, that the traditional separation of powers seemed threatened at its foundation. This is one of essential reasons for this scenario to the development of the concept of the 'welfare state'.

Now the phrase 'welfare state' has become a part of common parlance, but it was probably first used by Archbishop William Temple in his pamphlet 'Citizen and Churchman', published in 1941, in which he says:

"In place of the concept of power state we are led to that of the welfare state."

Regardless of its roots, a phenomenon that everyone understood as a duty by the government for the supply of social services fell into common use during the years after 1945. The term 'welfare state' reflects an attitude towards the state which sees it as a positive agent for the promotion of social welfare.[174]

174 Mamta Rao, Public Interest Litigation – Legal Aid and Lok Adalats 3 (Eastern Book Company, Lucknow, 4th edn., 2015).

8. COMPARATIVE OVERVIEW ACROSS THE GLOBE

UNITED KINGDOM

The Montesquieu doctrine was supported by the famous English Jurist Blackstone. As stated by him:

"Wherever the right of making & enforcing the law is vested in the same manner in the same body of men, there can be no liberty."

Parliament exercised constitutional authority in England throughout the seventeenth century. But with the creation of the cabinet regime of states, the King practiced executive powers whereas judicial powers were practiced by courts. The doctrine remains of no use in the representative system of government. The famous Bagehot Constitutional jurist observed:

"The cabinet is a hyphen which joins, a buckle which fastens the legislative part of the State to the executive part of the State."[175]

As stated by Wade and Phillips[176] the separation of powers doctrine states:

1. The government's one organ must not violate the functions of the other two organs.
2. The government's one organ must not exercise the functions of the other two organs.
3. The government's one organ should not encroach on the function of the other two organs of the Government.

175 E. C. S. Wade and G. Godfrey Phillips, Constitutional Law 22-34 (Longmans Green & Co., London, 6th edn., 1960).

176 *Ibid.*

UNITED STATES OF AMERICA

The separation of powers doctrine has been stated to be well-referred in the US Constitution, although it is not explicitly stated anywhere[177]. In his reliance on the Montesquieu doctrine, Madison the noted Federalist said:

"The accumulation of all powers legislative, executive and judicial, in the same hands whether of one, a few or many and whether hereditary, self-appointed or elective, may justly be pronounced as the very definition of tyranny."

In 1788, Hamilton expressed some similar ideas.

It has been observed in American Constitution that separate entities possess judicial, executive, and legislative powers.[178]

- Article I, Section 1 stated: "All legislative powers herein acknowledged shall be vested in a Congress of the United State".
- Article II, Section 1 stated: "The executive power shall be vested in a President of the United States of America."
- Article III, Section 1 stated: "The judicial power of the United States shall be vested in one Supreme Court & such inferior courts as the Congress may from time to time ordain and establish..."

As far as the judiciary is concerned, it monitors both Congress and the President as part of judicial review. It is correct that a statute is passed by the legislature, but it is often true that courts have to create the law in the case of new issues where the law is silent.

FRANCE

France had a dominant power in European affairs during the despotic regime of Louis XIV (1643-1715). Ludwig XIV had the same kingship as that the English people, and sought hopelessly to be recognized by

177 James Madison & Thomas Jefferson, The Constitution of the United States (CreateSpace Independent Publishing Platform, July 4, 2014)

178 Bernard Schwartz, American Constitutional Law (Cambridge [Eng.] University Press, 1955).

James I. The principle of Louis XIV was that without any doubts or critique the subject must follow the King in any way. He was named an autocrat tyrant because of this capricious action.

Montesquieu, one of the greatest intellectual authors of 18th-century, promoted his principle of separation of power based on the British Constitution; his doctrine of separation of powers is also contained in the French Declaration of Human Rights. Article 16 of this declaration, notes that without a division of authority, no democratic or constitutional government will exist. However, this effort has proven to be ineffective.[179]

THE 'SEPARATION OF POWERS' DOCTRINE: INDIAN PERSPECTIVE

In Constituent Assembly Debates Prof. K.T. Shah, a member of the Constituent Assembly laid emphasis to insert by amendment, a new Article 40-A concerned with the doctrine of separation of powers. This Article reads:

"There shall be a complete separation of powers between the principal organs of the State, viz; the legislative, the executive, and the judicial."[180]

The proposal (while Shri K. Hanumanthaiah, another member, dissented with the proposal of Prof. K.T. Shah) was fully agreed upon by Kazi Syed Karimuddin (a member of Constituent Assembly). He said that in his amendment Professor Shah and sponsors of the President's executive approved the parliamentary form of government that is appropriate for that region.

He elaborated more on:

"Instead of having a conflicting trinity, it is better to have a harmonious governmental structure. If we completely separate the Executive, the Judiciary, and the Legislature, conflicts are bound to arise between these three departments of Government. In any country or any government,

179 Richard Bellamy, The Political Form of the Constitution: The Separation of Powers, Rights and Representative Democracy, XLIV Political Studies 436-456 (1996)."

180 C. A. D. (Vol. VII) Book No.2, 959, Second Print, 1989.

conflicts are suicidal to the peace and progress of the country. Therefore, in a governmental structure, it is necessary to have what is called 'harmony' and not this three-fold conflict."[181]

Among the significant architects of the Indian Constitution, Dr. B.R. Ambedkar, who disagreed with Prof. K.T. Shah's argument stated:

"There is no dispute over whether that the Executive should be separated from the Judiciary. Concerning the separation of the Executive from the Legislature, such a separation does indeed exist in the Constitution of United States; but more Americans themselves were quite dissatisfied along with the rigid separation embodied in the American Constitution between Executive and the Legislature... There is not the slightest doubt in my mind and the minds of many students of Political Science, that the work of Parliament is so complicated, so vast that unless & until the members of the Legislature receive direct guidance and initiative from the members of the Executive, sitting in Parliament, it would be very difficult for Members of Parliament to carry on the work of the Legislature. I personally, therefore, do not think that any great loss is likely to occur if we do not adopt the US method of separating the Executive from the Legislature."[182]

The above findings also dismissed the motion for introducing a new Article 40-A concerning the separation of powers.

According to Montesquieu, constitutional administration means refusing every absolute authority of the State, while the fundamental basis of the constitutional government lies in the structure of checks and balances. His iconic declaration has become a fundamental law in every new constitutional democracy. However, when formulating the above proposal, the major characteristics that are essential for a coherent and uncomplicated governance system were not evident to him.

Furthermore, these essential significant characteristics comprise of:

1. A written constitution that determines its supremacy over the institutions established beneath it.

181 Ibid.

182 *Id.* at 967, 968.

2. Power distribution between the State's three organs.
3. The status of co-equality, as well as the coordination of powers between the three organs.

The essence of the doctrine of 'Separation of powers' regarding the Judiciary was explained by Prof. D.D. Basu a well-known Constitutional scholar, as[183]:

"So far as the courts are concerned, the application of the doctrine may involve two propositions: namely

i. *That none of the three organs of Government, Legislative Executive, and Judicial, can exercise any power that properly belongs to either of the other two.*

ii. *That the Legislature cannot "delegate its powers."*

In his address to the Constituent Assembly, Dr. B.R. Ambedkar also shared his views on the authority tests carried out by the different government bodies. To say the following:

"The purpose of a Constitution is not merely to create the organs of the State but to limit their authority, because, if no limitation is imposed upon the authority of the organs, there will be complete tyranny and complete oppression... It would result in utter chaos."[184]

Although Indian Constitution doesn't expressly address the same, it provides for a system of government that builds upon the division of powers. For example, the executive authority of the union is expressly delegated by Article 53(1), and where Article 50 states that 'the State shall take action in the public services to disconnect the judge from the Executive.'

The *Separation of Power* in the Indian sense is one of the fundamental characteristics of our Constitution that the Supreme Court, in *State of Bihar v. Bal Mukund Sha*[185], has rightly declared.

183 *Id.* at 967, 968.
184 C. A. D. (Vol. IX) 1659-63.
185 (2000) 4 SCC 640.

Vithal Bhai Patel, who headed the then Central Legislative Assembly, was insisting on the separation of powers. He demanded that the executive, legislative, and judiciary be divided. The British were unable to acknowledge this plan, but proclaimed on the House's floor:

"As the elected President, I announce that Motilal Nehru will move a resolution for such a separation and Lala Lajpat Rai will second the resolution".[186]

The bill, that set background for division of authority, was unexpectedly accepted overwhelmingly. Nevertheless, the Constitution of India doesn't allow for an absolute division of powers, as in the USA, because certain members of the legislative branch are still members of the Government in India by being ministers. The Constitution, however, explicitly sets out limits for any organ that must not be breached.

In *Indira Nehru Gandhi v. Raj Narain*[187], the Supreme Court observed that the separation of powers is a basic feature of the Constitution. The topic of the partition of powers appeared before the Supreme Court, and in its classic and rigid sense, the doctrine of separation of power was not embraced.

The Indian Constitution had however managed to separate each of the organs from the powers of the other State Departments. That is expressed quite well in the numerous constitutional clauses such as:

Article 121 - it puts a kind of restriction on Parliament. It states that no discussion shall take place in Parliament with respect to the conduct of any Judge of the Supreme Court or a High Court in the discharge of his duties.

Article 211 - it contains a similar provision for the State legislatures.

Furthermore, the doctrine was reinforced in the constitution as stated by Article 122:

---

186 Madhu Dandavate, Legacy of the Presiding Officers of Parliament, Dr. Yogendra Narain (ed.), Role and Relevance of Rajya Sabha in Indian Polity 11 (Rajya Sabha Secretariat, New Delhi, 2004)."

187 AIR 1975 SC 2299.

'Courts not to inquire into proceedings of Parliament:

1. The validity of any proceedings in Parliament shall not be called in question on the ground of any alleged irregularity of procedure
2. No officer or member of Parliament in whom powers are vested by or under to this Constitution for regulating procedure or the conduct of business, or for maintaining order, in Parliament shall be subject to the jurisdiction of any court in respect of the exercise by him of those powers.'

Thus, Articles 212 and 122 have equally prohibited the courts to inquiring into the Legislature as well as the Parliament's proceedings respectively.

Also, the Governor or the President has immunity of a certain kind under Article 361. It provides that the President or Governor is not answerable to any judge for the exercise as well as enforcement of powers of his office along with the duties.

Moreover, Article 74(2) mandates that the question of whether any and if so, what advice was tendered by Ministers to the President shall not be inquired into by any court.

These clauses are sufficiently demonstrative to infer that, the constitutional makers have taken every practicable measure to have a robust form of separation of powers under the Indian constitutional scheme, and thereby preserve the freedom of each state entity and, at the same time, maintain the 'checks and balance' process to uphold the flag of rule of law.

Subsequently, in *I.C. Golak Nath & Ors. v. State of Punjab & Anr,*[188] the Supreme Court re-affirmed its view with regards to separation of powers in the following words:

"The Constitution creates the Legislature; the Executive and the Judiciary demarcates to the jurisdiction minutely. It expects them to exercise their respective powers without overstepping their limits. They should function within the spheres allotted to them."

188 AIR 1967 SC 1643

The idea of the welfare state originated during the twentieth century, which strengthened interaction among parts of the government and its functionaries. It was essentially divided into three wings, namely the judiciary, the executive, and the legislature, to avoid the concentration of authority in one organ of the government.

The theory of separation of powers stated that they must always be kept separate in a free democracy. Each should act in its sphere i.e., the Legislature cannot exercise executive or judicial power, the Executive cannot interfere in legislative or judicial power, & the Judiciary cannot exercise legislative or executive powers of the government. But it should be noted that nowadays the implication of the doctrine of separation of powers in its true sense is not possible because enforcement of rigid conception of separation of powers would make the modern government impossible. This has led to a frantic situation where the three types of machinery of the state now trying to overpower each other.

Separation of Powers, propounded by the French political thinker Montesquieu, has been elaborated in the judgment delivered in *Divisional Manager, Aravali Golf Club v. Chander Hass & Anr.*[189]

Judicial activism is a deviation from this principle. Judicial activism is based on the theory of Jurisprudence called Sociological Jurisprudence, which arms the Judiciary with wide legislative and executive powers.

This delicate balancing among the three state institutions has been illustrated in the decision by the Supreme Court in the case of the *State of U.P. v. Jeet S. Bisht*[190]. The topic of judicial activism against judicial control has entered the discourse on the separation of powers doctrine.

In this famous decision, Justice Markandey Katju and Justice S.B. Sinha former judges of the Supreme Court of India stated their completely opposing viewpoints. Furthermore, it has opined by Justice S.B. Sinha:[191]

---

189 (2008) 1 SCC 683 (vide paragraphs 17 to 40

190 (2007) 6 SCC 586.

191 Ibid.

"20. The judge-made law is now well recognized throughout the world. If one is to put the doctrine of separation of power to such rigidity, it would not have been possible for any superior court of any country, whether developed or developing, to create new rights through the interpretative process.

21. Separation of power in one sense is a limit on the active jurisdiction of each organ. But it has other deeper and more relevant purpose: to act as a check and balance to the activities of other organs. Thereby the active jurisdiction of the organ is not challenged; nevertheless, there are methods of prodding to communicate the institution of its excesses and shortfall in duty. Constitutional mandate sets the dynamics of this communication among the organs of the polity. Therefore, it is suggested to not understand Separation of Power as operating in a vacuum. Separation of power doctrine is reinvented in modern times."

Justice Katju's trenchant and forthright views as an integral part of this ongoing debate, were:[192]

"47. Under our Constitution, the Judiciary, the Legislature, and the Executive are bound to their broad spheres of operation. These organs must not encroach on each other's demarcated spheres and confine themselves to their own; otherwise, there will always be danger of a reaction. Of the three organs of the State, it is only Judiciary that has right to determine the limits of the jurisdiction of all these three organs. This great power should therefore be exercised by the Judiciary with the most humility and self-restraint.

48. The Judiciary must therefore exercise self-restraint and avoid the temptation to encroach into the domain of the Legislature or the administrative or statutory authorities. By exercising self-restraint, it will enhance its respect and prestige. Of course, if a law violates some provision of the Constitution, it can be struck down, but otherwise, it is not for the Court to sit in appeal over the wisdom of the Legislature, nor can it amend the law."

In the constitutional jurisprudence in India, the concept of separation of powers has a strong footing. This can be seen from the

192 *Ibid.*

observations of the Supreme Court in *State of West Bengal & Ors. v. Committee for protection of Democratic Rights, West Bengal & Ors.*[193]

"It is true that in the Constitutional scheme adopted in India, besides supremacy of the Constitution, the separation of powers between the Legislature, the Executive & the Judiciary constitutes the basic features of the Constitution."

A judge simply applies the law that it gets from the legislature as a corollary of the doctrine of the separation of powers. The Anglo-Saxon legal practice has thus stressed that the judge represents rule solely irrespective of expected results, justice considerations, or public policy. He isn't empowered to legislate.

In this respect, Dr. Surat Singh has examined the prevailing developments in the judgments of the Supreme Court over the previous five decades, as under:[194]

"Period of excessive difference towards legislative and executive wings of the government (1950 to 1966); Zealous protector of fundamental rights; self-declared protector of fundamental values of the Constitution; The implementation of Basic Structure theory against Smt. Indira Gandhi herself (1976); The dark period of Emergency and the retreat of Judiciary in its cell; Post-emergency liberal interpretation of traditional standards of locus standi.; The Supreme Court in search of its identity - exploring the potential with limitation of its role (the late 1980s); Attaining the maturity with asserting its self-importance (mid-1990s)."

On 10 December 2007, when the two judges' bench consisting of Justice Markandey Katju and A.K. Mathur criticized the tendency of Judicial Liberalism betraying overreach that was evident to them in two earlier rulings of the Supreme Court itself, and thereby the Supreme Court added a new chapter to this dispute.[195]The Court held that creation, sanction of posts is a prerogative of the executive or legislative

193 AIR 2010 SC 1476.

194 Dr Surat Singh, Judicial Activism – How Wise, How Otherwise, K.M Bishwajit Bhattacharyya (Ed.), Judging the Judges 133-140 (Gyan Publication House, New Delhi, 1999)."

195 Prof. Virendra Kumar, Judges v. Judges, The Tribune (New Delhi), Dec. 21, 2007." 231 AIR 1980 SC 1789, 1981 SCR (1) 206.

authorities, and the court can't assume to itself this purely executive or legislative function and directly create post in any organization. The learned judges, referring to Montesquieu, said that it is not right for either of three bodies to interfere in another's jurisdiction, or else the fragile equilibrium of the Constitution will be disturbed, or a reaction will arise.

Article 122 of the Indian Constitution declares that, based on any perceived procedural irregularity, a Court cannot call in question any proceedings of the parliament. Although Article 212 stipulates that Court shall not enquire into the proceedings of the Legislature, in recent times such judicial anomalies have been felt. The notable case was the 1998 case of *Jagdambika Pal* involving the Assembly of Uttar Pradesh and the 2005 Jharkhand Assembly matter. The interim order of the Supreme Court in both cases is a clear violation of the principle of separation of powers between Judiciary & Legislature. The Judiciary blames Legislature for not making anything worthwhile over the past three decades, whereas Legislature accuses Judiciary of doing the job of the Legislature. When courts are not kept responsible for the statutory duties, it is not wrong to question their legitimacy after all.

These examples show that there has been a constant tussle of amendment power in favour of Parliament and sometimes Judiciary. The Parliament's Forty-second Amendment Act resulted in a dramatic amendment to the Constitution's provisions. Through the change, Article 368, which grants Parliament amending rights, was revised in such a manner that any additional constitutional amendment will be immune from being questioned before the Court of Law. The power tilted in favour of the Legislature.

The Supreme Court as reply held in, Minerva Mills v. Union of India[196]that that 'judicial review' as a central characteristic of the constitution is not to be abolished by the parliament by amendment of the Constitution.

In comparison, the judiciary has played the role of a legislature without taking the real challenge and financial limitations into account. It is not just the recommendations but strategies that have

196 AIR 1980 SC 1789, 1981 SCR (1) 206.

been established. The fundamental theory of democracy is that authority is both in and out of persons as such responsibility to the public as a whole is a key to democracy's progress and survival in its varied ways. In the Preamble itself (that is also the basis of all governing institutions), the fundamental importance of the people's will, find its greatest representation in the following words: *"We, the people of India"* and *"do hereby adopt, enact and give to ourselves this Constitution"*.

Justice V.S. Sirpurkar and Justice Markandey Katju declined to grant a decree of divorce on the grounds of a breakdown in the union on 11 March 2009 in *Vishnu Dutt Sharma v. Manju Sharma*[197], where they observed:

"If we grant a divorce on this ground, then we shall by judicial verdict be adding a clause to section 13 of the Hindu Marriage Act, 1955. In our opinion, this can be done only by the Legislature and not by the court."

Surprisingly, however, prior courts have granted a divorce for similar reasons. In the 21st century, the Supreme Court took full advantage of its potential and acknowledged its limitations.[198]

The relation between the executive as well as the judiciary has consistently been a sensitive topic. A rule of law-based society still requires that the judiciary be isolated from the Executive. And yet, the rule of law is still open to the possibility that the executive will infringe. In this case, the proper functioning of democracy demands a strong distinction between the two. The primary role of a judge is to conduct the justice system without fear and favour, which cannot be properly administered without a separation of the judiciary from the executive. The framers of the Constitution wanted to enact amendments whenever possible – simultaneously with no delay; and where this concept cannot be immediately applied, they were nonetheless intended to be recognized as a duty imperative.

In principle, separations between the Judiciary & the Executive are often a welcome measure. The goal is always for ensuring that the

197 Editorial, Irretrievable breakdown is no ground for divorce, The Hindu (Delhi) March 12, 2009."

198 I.R. Coelho (dead) by LRs v. State of Tamil Nadu & Ors (2007) 2 SCC1: AIR 2007 SC 861

judiciary doesn't resolve cases under the influence of the government but respects the concept of rule of law. However, the main issue is one of separation. That is a challenge. The position of judges under the British rules had already alerted the framers of Indian Constitution about the judiciary's inherent constraints. Chapter IV of Part V of our Constitution, on judicial affairs in the Union, allows for a strong bond between the judiciary & the legislative body.

In numerous occurrences as part of the Constitution's fundamental features, the sovereignty of the Constitution, representative government, the concept of divorcing states, the freedom of the courts, the minimal changes to the Parliament, etc. are often matters of lengthy discussion. In this regard, all state agencies must carefully analyse diverse viewpoints as well as guarantee that the requirements of the Constitution are not infringed. They must therefore make attempts to reinforce the relations between the two institutions, for the integrity of the whole framework of our political structure would be jeopardized if any institution is undermined.

Correspondingly, the Supreme Court in *Rai Sahib Ram Jawaya Kapur and Ors. v. The State of Punjab*[199], reflecting on the essence of the separation of powers outlining this Constitution, found the Executive qualified to make laws under Article 162; as observed by Supreme Court:

> *"12... The Indian Constitution has not indeed recognized the doctrine of separation of powers in its absolute rigidity although the functions of the different parts or branches of the Government is sufficiently differentiated and consequently, it can very well be said that the Constitution doesn't contemplate assumption, by one organ or part of the State, of functions that essentially belong to another."*

It is safe to assume that the 2005 *Jharkhand Assembly* case and in 1998 in *Jagdambika Pal* case[200], which involved the Uttar-Pradesh legislative assembly and, the variations in the constitutionality scheme are widely recognized. Many perceived the concept of 'composite

199 AIR 1955 SC 549: 1955 SCA 577: 1955 SCJ 504."

200 Jagdambika Pal v. Union of India, (1999) 9 SCC 95: AIR 1998 SC 998: 1998 AIR SCW 767."

floor-test' introduced by the Supreme Court in the 1998 and 2005 cases, as an avoidable interference with the powers & privileges of the Legislature by the Judiciary.

The government and several individuals of public interest have regarded both the decisions of the Supreme Court in *Nandini Sundar v. State of Chhattisgarh*[201] (Nandini Sundar) and *Ram Jethmalani v. Union of India*[202] as acts outside constitutional borders, which cross the barrier of the separation of powers and result in judicial overlaps.

The doctrine represents mostly the determination of the court to delay, or not postpone, any governmental action. Katju pointed out in a friendly and stern warning to the courts that courts sometimes refuse to grasp their boundaries.

"Apart from the doctrine of separation of powers, courts should realize there are many problems in the country which courts cannot solve, however much they like to…" he said.

"The country can hardly afford to be governed through court decrees."

The Judges instructed the Judiciary for dispensing justice in compliance with the constitution & law, and any attempt to pass such writs/orders would not only be 'grossly undemocratic' but would be riskier as courts may not have experience or tools in that regard.

"He cannot ask other branches of the State to keep within their Constitutional limits if he exceeds his own", as by a famous saying's quoting, "Who will guard the Praetorian guards?"[203]

Deciding on an appeal filed by a Haryana golf club where to the court produced practically a work, saying:

"Judiciary should confine itself to its proper sphere, realizing that in democracy more matters and controversies are best resolved in non-judicial setting...Judges must know to their limits and must not try to run the

201 (2011) 7 SCC 547: (2011) 2 SCC (L&S) 762.
202 (2011) 8 SCC 1: (2011) 3 SCC (Cri) 310.
203 Court Monitoring Committees is Illegal – available at http://archive. Indianexpress.com/news/court-monitoring-committees-illegal... stop-pilblackmailjustice-katju-slams-his-own/295916/

Government. They must have modesty and humility, and not behave like Emperors."[204]

No obstacle can be encountered in embracing judicial constraint or moral centrism as a theory of justice itself. But this ideology varies considerably from that of ethical advocacy. Withstanding the seeming terms, 'judicial restraint' only ensures that the judge keeps to the rules and decides on legal issues solely in line with established principles of law without encroaching the constitutionally forbidden territories reserved for another branch of the government. That precisely is the role a Judge that is called upon to play because of the oath that he undertakes. A Judge is not free to render justice as he thinks but is required to render justice *according to the law.*

It has been appropriately commented in an editorial by the Times of India:

"Judges are meant to act as humble interpreters of the law, not pose as emperors who adjudicate on a whim. We need faceless, impassive Judges, compassionate but disciplined legislators, and an Executive that acknowledges the supremacy of the Legislature and independence of the Judiciary. Sadly, technical-Judges are not an easy sight in India. While some arrange marriages between rapists and their victims, others turn into committed municipal authorities. Courts are meant to be more serious than Bollywood makes them out to be."[205]

FINDINGS

It can be inferred that the concept of division of power faces constant scrutiny since there is a lot of anxiety voiced by participants in the active discussion regarding the judges who take over the functions of the executive & the legislature. In fostering fairness and impartiality in the implementation of penalties, the distinction is essential. The executive will represent their private benefit and the bias of the officials who charge the penalties, and their policies may therefore be volatile as they have the authority to determine if they will be penalized.

---

204 *Ibid.*

205 Editorial, "The Interpreters: Judiciary Shouldn't Stray from The Rule Book, The Times of India, Sept. 17, 2005."

However, when laws are standardized and drawn up by officials who find it impossible to estimate the impact of the provisions in individual situations on their objectives, it is more probable that the policies enacted represents a large social estimation about suitable policies than the private benefit of officers themselves.

It can be argued that citizens themselves don't want to see any particular entity. Many times, citizens have struggled against the supremacy of the government they have selected. It is important to provide some value to the fact that no organization is strong enough to walk over on the interests of its people. Each system has its own set of limitations.

The division process & the balance of forces must be in effect in each organization. When the scale tilts to one side, citizens are struggling tremendously because the stronger organization is autocratic. The new definition of constitutionalism allows the government to act solely in compliance with the Federal requirements. According to John Locke, the ideology of the triumphant English Revolution (1688) that created a parliamentary monarchy was its greatest representative. Constitutionalism thus counters arbitrariness by restricting each wing's control.

9. POST-EMERGENCY GROWTH OF JUDICIAL ACTIVISM

"The inn that shelters for the night is not the journey's end. The law, like the traveller, must be ready for tomorrow.

It must have a principle of growth."206

After the emergency was lifted, it began to be clear that choices such as *Kesavananda* were relevant and thus the provision of the review was generally important. The post emergency era is occasionally called as 'Judicial Activism era' because Supreme Court could be seen separating itself from legal positivism.

THE APEX COURT'S JURISDICTIONAL EXPANSION

The examination of public law was not restricted strictly to upholding public rights; rather in India, it was expanded to establish proper control over administrative acts.

The Supreme Court is the *"sentinel on the qui vive"* in which the constitutionally protected fundamental rights exist and bear meaning and life. It has thus tremendously extended its jurisdiction to include the authorities traditionally considered beyond the court's written competence. The Commission have also expanded its jurisdictional reach by making a public law remedy available to victims not only against the State but against individuals too.

In addition to the rights of working women, the right of all general workers related to employment, advancement as well as other occupational consequences, must progressively be secured from various public enterprises and institutions.[207]

The State will be forced for ensuring that rights of the workers are not encroached by such bodies. The liberal understanding of the

---

206 Cardozo Benjamin N, The Growth of Law 19, 20 (Yale university Press, New Heaven, 1924)."

207 Kapila Hingorani (1) v. State of Bihar, (2003) 6 SCC 1; Kapila Hingorani (2) v. State of Bihar, (2005) 2 SCC 262; 2005 SCC (L&S) 206.

word 'State' as established by Article 12 of the Constitution has been provided by the Supreme Court against that perspective.

The first move to increase the Supreme Court's jurisdiction became evident when the Court left the conventional principle *'ejusdem generis'* and developed the principle of Constitutional or legislative authority granted by law in *Rajasthan SEB v. Mohan Lal*[208]. Under Article 12, the word 'other authorities' necessarily meant an entity engaged in the State's sovereign functions.

The Supreme Court's jurisdictional reach further broadened by evolution of the concept of state agency or its instrumentality, that was expanded in *Ramana Dayaram Shetty v. International Airport Authority of India* (R.D. Shetty)[209]. It discussed whether the International Airport Authority was an agency or instrumentality of the State, to provide the security of fundamental rights to its employees by a three-judge Bench composed of Bhagwati, Pathak, and Tulzapurkar JJ.

In *Ajay Hasia v. Khalid Mujib Sehravardi*[210] (Ajay Hasia), the court took a more drastic measure to extend the jurisdiction of the Court. The test that was proposed by Mathew J in *Sukhdev Singh*[211] and Bhagwati J in *R.D. Shetty*[212] was reformulated by the constitutional bench in *Ajay Hasia.*

It addressed the challenge of admissions to a school founded and administered by a company that is registered under the J&K Registration of Societies Act, 1898, in a petition under Article 32 of the Constitution. Bhagwati J provided a new viewpoint to explain the increased competence of the court. He said:

"It is immaterial for this purpose whether the corporation is created by a statute or under a statute. The test is whether it is an instrumentality or agency of the Government and not as to how it is created. The inquiry has

208 AIR 1967 SC 1857: (1967) 3 SCR 377.
209 (1979) 3 SCC 489: AIR 1979 SC 1628
210 (1981) 1 SCC 722: AIR 1981 SC 487.
211 (1975) 1 SCC 421: 1975 SCC (L&S) 101
212 (1979) 3 SCC 489: AIR 1979 SC 1628

to be not as to how the juristic person is born but why it has been brought into existence."[213]

A three-judge bench ruled in *Som Prakash Rekhi v. Union of India*[214] (Som Prakash Rekhi) on the day *Ajay Hasia* was decided. Krishna Iyer J (for himself and Reddy J) took the majority decision and Pathak J passed a separate verdict. Krishna Iyer J in *Som Prakash Rekhi* followed a similar line of thought as adopted by Bhagwati J in *Ajay Hasia*[215]. Krishna J Iyer said that it was immaterial to declare the Bharat Petroleum Corporation to be a "State," within the context of Article 12, or to assess whether the company was created by legislation or a statute. He stressed the following:

"The true test is functional. Not how the legal person is born but why it is created."

A seven-judge bench of the Supreme Court, comprising S.P. Bharucha CJ, S.S. Mohammad Quadri, R.C. Lahoti, S. Santosh Hegde, Doraiswamy Raju, Ruma Pal, and Arijit Pasayat JJ, in *Pradeep Kumar Biswas v. Indian Institute of Chemical Biology*[216] by a majority of 5:2, declared the Council of Scientific and Industrial Research (CSIR) an instrumentality of the State and, thereby, brought it within the definition of "State" under Article 12. R. C. Lahoti J dissented and wrote the dissenting judgment for himself and Doraiswamy Raju J.

EXPANSION OF SCOPE OF ARTICLE 21

The Indian Constitution adopted after independence, like other democratic constitutions, ensured Fundamental Rights to their citizens. Democracy cannot be established in any case, until some minimal rights, essential for existence, are assured to every citizen of the country. These aspirations are depicted in the Constitution's Preamble as well as Part III that offers such rights for each resident within Indian territories.

213 *Id.* at para 11.
214 (1981) 1 SCC 449: AIR 1982 SC 212.
215 (1981) 1 SCC 722: AIR 1981 SC 487.
216 2002(3) SCALE 638, (2002) 5 SCC 111, 3 SCR 100.

Part III, dealing with Fundamental Rights, composes a *pattern of guarantee* for a basic human rights system along with imposing negative obligations on the State to prevent any encroachment on various dimensions of individual liberty. At the same time, the judicial approach to understanding the right to personal freedom under Article 21 has also changed from a limited viewpoint towards a far broader approach.

The Constitution's Part III incorporates the right to life as well as rights of individuals in various phases of evolution.

Restructured Article 21 is an offshoot of the Supreme Court of India's legal dynamism and advocacy. The Supreme Court's democratic growth as a protector of the rights of the people is the most significant & substantial change in independent India's judicial history. It is not considered to be an affluent society redress platform, but a place whereby citizens who are deprived, marginalized, oppressed by the misuse of powers, women and children, victims of exploitation, and environmental groups, as well as roles, are brought forward, remedied, and expressed.

The *Maneka Gandhi's case*[217] came as a big breakthrough. It was a notable example of the extension of the legislation to improve personal and fundamental rights. In this case, passport law has been construed in a way that limits the right of personal freedom and personal liberty.

Maneka Gandhi's passport had been impounded and she challenged the validity of the action on the ground that it violated her personal liberty. There was no hearing on why she shouldn't enforce her passport, and the Supreme Court not only gave wider meaning to the words 'personal liberty' but also brought in the concept of 'procedural due process'. While the term 'personal freedom' has a broader sense, the Court held that previous view of 'personal freedom,' along with all the characteristics of freedom except those referred in Article 19, was rejected. Where a law limits personal freedom, a court may further consider whether such limitation, also imposed limitations on any of the rights laid down in Article 19.

217 Maneka Gandhi v. Union of India 1978 AIR 597: 1978 SCR (2) 621: 1978 SCC (1) 248

Article 19 also includes certain rights that directly indicate an individual's fundamental freedom. The court in *Maneka Gandhi* held that traveling abroad also formed part of the freedom of the citizen. The Court governs that its passport imposition without a hearing did not adhere to legal procedures. There must be a fair and just process.

The *'rules of natural justice'*, formulates the basic conditions of a fair procedure essential for carrying out rational hearings. The following are the rules:

1. Nobody must be condemned unheard; and
2. Nobody must be a judge in his own cause.

In the case, Court was called upon to decide whether Mrs. Maneka Gandhi was entitled to a hearing before to her passport was impounded. The court conceded that a preliminary hearing might not be possible in some cases where immediate action is needed. The authorities must hold a post-decisional hearing in such extraordinary circumstances if a pre-hearing was not held. The majority, except Justice Beg, observed that the government's action need not be stuck down. Justice Beg held the Government's action as unconstitutional and void.

The Gopalan case was overruled by Court in *Maneka Gandhi* based on the following issues:

- The law authorizing deprivation of personal liberty would have to be valid not only under Article 21 but also under Article 19(1)(d).

- The words 'personal freedom' and 'life' had a larger sense that could be identified from time to time.

- The words 'procedure established by law' did not mean law-laid procedure, although in civilized countries, it was construed as just and fair.

The most critical feature of the *Maneka Gandhi case* was the seminal theory of constitutional interpretation laid down by the Court. It explained that the terms in the Constitution cannot be viewed solely in a textual manner. These words have deep meanings, which are interpreted in the light of the given circumstances. In the present case, it felt like the Pandora's Box was opened, resulting in the flooding of disagreements and the expansion of Article 21.

In *Minerva Mills Ltd. v. Union of India*[218], the scope and extent of implementation of the 'basic structure doctrine' were re-examined. In this case, the petitioners challenge the validity of Sections 4 and 55 of the Constitution (Forty-second Amendment) Act, 1976 on the ground of violation of the basic structure of the Constitution as laid down in *Kesavananda Bharati*. Articles 31-C and 368 respectively were amended by those portions. In the case of infringement of Articles 14, 19, and 21, the laws enforcing any Directive Principle were exempted from the appeal. In Article 368, paragraphs (4) and (5) have authenticated and removed any potential limits on future amendments which were previously invalidated or existed in standing amendments. Whilst a change to Article 368 was invalidated by the Court unanimously, a change to Article 31-C was invalidated by 4:1.

Applying the basic structure doctrine to Article 368, it was held:

"Since the Constitution had conferred a limited amending power on the Parliament, the Parliament cannot under the exercise of that limited power enlarge that appropriate power into absolute power. Indeed, limited amending power is one of the basic features of our Constitution and therefore, limitations on the power cannot be destroyed".[219]

Further, while adjudicating in *Waman Rao v. Union of India*[220], the 9th Schedule, Article31A, and Article31B's originality and revision's validity were considered in the light of the basic structure. The Court told that instead of weakening, the amendment strengthens the basic structure because it "made the Constitutional ideal of equal justice a living truth."[221] The Court also said same thing about the unamended Article 31-C as it stood before the Constitution (Forty-second Amendment) Act, 1976.

---

218 AIR 1980 SC 1789: 1981 SCR (1) 206.

219 *Ibid*

220 (1981) 2 SCC 362, 1981 2 SCR 1

221 *Ibid.*

ARTICLE 32 AND THE SUPREME COURT

Unless there is a suitable framework for its compliance, the guarantee of fundamental rights in the Constitution is meaningless. It is the proper implementation, which makes the right a reality. There exists no right if it is not implemented. Therefore, under Articles 32 and 226 of the Constitution, the founding fathers of Constitution defined an efficient mechanism for implementing such rights.

Article 32 provides recourse for the protection of the Constitution's privileges under Part III. The remedy under Article 32 has been defined to be available only in violation of the guaranteed Fundamental Rights. In the light of the Supreme Court's liberalized view of the meaning of Article 21, a new approach has been established for protecting the rights of an accused individual. The power of the Supreme Court to deviate from traditional concepts and formulate new rules for granting effective relief for violation of fundamental rights can be traced back to Article 32.

Considering the ambit of Article 32(1), in *Bandhua Mukti Morcha*[222] Bhagwati, J. noted:

"There is no limitation concerning the nature of proceeding envisaged in Article 32(1) except that the proceeding must be 'appropriate', and this requirement of appropriateness must be judged in the light of the ambition for which the proceeding is to be taken, namely, enforcement of a fundamental right. The Constitution-makers deliberately didn't lay down every form of proceeding for the enforcement of a fundamental right. They didn't stipulate that such proceeding should conform to any rigid pattern or straitjacket formula as in England.

They knew that in a country like in India where there is so much of poverty, ignorance, illiteracy, deprivation and exploitation, any insistence on a rigid formula of proceeding for the enforcement of a fundamental right, would become self-defeating and it would place enforcement of fundamental rights beyond the reach of the common man. The entire remedy for enforcement of fundamental rights which the Constitution-makers regarded as so precious and invaluable, and elevated to the status

222 Bandhua Mukti Morcha v. Union of India, (1984) 3 SCC 161

of the fundamental right, would become a mere rope of sand so far as the large masses of the people of this country are concerned."

The Court can grant *appropriate* remedies to enforce the rights within the purview of Article 32(2). The authority can thus be traced to be an 'appropriate' remedy under Article 32(2) of the Indian Constitution.

The Court in *Bandhua Mukti Morcha's* case emphasized that while interpreting the Article, the approach must be guided, not by any verbal or formalistic canons of construction but by the paramount object with the purpose that the Article and its interpretation must receive illumination alongside the trinity of provisions which permeate and energize the entire Constitution viz. the preamble, fundamental rights & directive principles of State policy.

The Supreme Court, regarding the power of the court to enforce fundamental rights, observed:

"It is not only the entitled writs of mandamus, habeas corpus, prohibition, quo warranto & certiorari which can be issued by the Supreme Court but also if the pre-requisite conditions concerning these writs are not fulfilled, the Supreme Court would not be constrained to fold its hands in despair & plead its inability to help the citizen who has come before it for judicial redress, but would have power to issue any direction, order or writ including a writ like any high prerogative writ."[223]

EVOLUTION OF COMPENSATORY JURISPRUDENCE

The interpretation of Article 21 by the Indian Judiciary is not only the challenging duty of the day, where it is imperative to take a substantive and coherent approach to the compensatory case law, but also requires adjudicating in harmony with the spirit of the Constitution.

After 1977, numerous cases involving wrongful detention and death of a prisoner in custody, reached the Supreme Court by way of writ petitions under Article 32 of the Constitution or in appeals against decisions of the High Court under Article 226 of the Constitution. Where the arrest was found to be unconstitutional or that a custodial

223 *Id.* at 187-88, para 13.

death happened due to ill-treatment or gross negligence on the part of police officers, compensation was given to the injured individual (or to his legal representatives).

Through these provisions, the claimant can not only expeditiously enforce his rights but can also demand compensation for the infringement of the fundamental right by the State.

Justice Bhagwati encountered the issue of compensation in *Khatri v. State of Bihar*[224], commonly referred to as the Bhagalpur blinding case. Articles 21 and 32 of the Constitution were accorded new meanings as the Court directed the State to cover the housing expenses of blind homes in Delhi. The Court asked whether the grant of monetary relief would compensate an individual for the deprivation by the state of the right to life or personal freedom. Here, the Supreme Court had to examining whether its prison officers were responsible for blinding the inmates in Bhagalpur.

Furthermore, it has been affirmatively answered by Bhagwati, J. through a counter, thus:

"Why should the court not be prepared to forge new tool and devise new remedies to vindicate the most precious of the precious fundamental right to life and personal liberty?" [225]

As for the State's duty for paying compensations for the violation of Article 21, the Court responded affirmatively that, if it were not so, Article 21 will be stripped of its substantial significance. The Court further noted that where the primary Constitutional relevance requires an analysis of the personal liberty with a new dimension of right to life, in the light of the complex constitutional case law in which the Court has developed, it must assess the correct consequences of the Constitutional law under Article 21.

It directed the government of Bihar to forward all the blind prisoners to the All-India Institute of Medical Sciences, New Delhi.

224 1981 AIR 1068 1981 SCR (3) 145 1981 SCC (2) 493 1981 SCALE (1)531.

225 *Ibid.*

This provided for medical relief at the expense of the state as an exercise of its sovereign function.

A new dimension was introduced to the judicial activism in *Rudul Sah v. State of Bihar*[226]. It raised a variety of very significant issues such as the State's responsibility to indemnify arbitrary incarceration, the prospect of seeking compensation against the State for wrongful deprivation of fundamental rights through Article 32, and the propriety of Supreme Court for granting compensation to a *habeas corpus* petition to enforce the right to personal freedom. For more than fourteen years, the petitioner Rudal Sah was illegally detained in prison. For its immediate release, he lodged a Habeas Corpus before the court and, inter alia, demanded rehabilitation, wellbeing, and wrongful detention reparations. The point to discuss before the Court was whether the court can or cannot grant a compensatory order under Article 32 in the exercise of competence; and whether such an order was in the essence of compensation due to the deprivation of basic rights. The court replied affirmatively to this issue. This became a major catalyst in Indian legal history towards compensatory-cum-constitutional misconduct.

The decision in the *Rudal Sah* case was important in two respects:

- That infringement of a Constitutional right could result in enforcing the State' to perform its duty, by a civil court.
- It laid the groundwork for an accountability principle that may give rise to State's liability in matters related to the infringement of the right to personal freedom.

The decision was taken to preserve and safeguard the constitutional rights of a citizen from a non-sovereign and sovereign dichotomy.

Furthermore, the *locus classicus* is the judgment of the Supreme Court, where the petitioner detenue complained after his release by the Sessions court, that his detention for fourteen years was illegal.

The Court through Chandrachud C.J., ruled while analysing the State affidavit of this grave injustice perpetrated upon the petitioner:

226 1983 AIR 1086: 1983 SCR (3) 508: 1983 SCC (4) 141: 1983 SCALE (2)103.

"We see no effective answer to it, save the stale and sterile objection that the petitioner may if so advised, file a suit to recover the damages against the State Government. The petitioner could have consigned to the ordinary remedy of a suit if his compensation claim was factually in question in the sense that a civil court may or may not upheld his claim... In these circumstances, the refusal of this Court to pass an order of compensation in favour of the petitioner will be doing mere lip service ..."

"The extensive question for our consideration is whether, in the exercise of its jurisdiction under Article 32, can this Court pass an order for the payment of money, if the nature of such an order is like compensation."

Also, Court observed that, if the jurisdiction of the Court was restricted to the passage of order from an unlawful detention, Article 21 must be uncovered to reveal its underlying substance.

Furthermore, the Supreme Court expressed:

"One of the effective ways in which the violation of that right can reasonably be prevented is through securing a due compliance mandate of Article 21, is to direct its violators in the payment of monetary compensation. Administrative sclerosis leading to flagrant infringements of fundamental rights cannot be corrected by any other method open to the judiciary to adopt."

"The right to compensation is somewhat palliative against, those unlawful acts of instrumentalities which act in the name of public interest, and also acts as shield against the abuse of powers by the state. If civilization is not to perish in this country as it has in some, too well-known to mention, it is necessary to educate the individuals into accepting that respect of the rights of everyone in a sovereign state is the true bastion of democracy. Therefore, the state must make do for the damage done by its officers to the petitioner's rights. It may have recourse against those officers."[227]

However, the amount of compensation being Rs. 35,000, is too meager to 'mulct' the violators, and it is doubtful whether it would at all, assist Rudul Sah to pursue his rights through the convoluted judiciary (because the Indian legal profession is a market for sellers), the Court has been observant to make innovations, and every move in

227 Rudul Sah v. State of Bihar 1983 SCC (4) 141 at 147-48

the direction of judicial justice seems *essential.*[228] On this point, it has been noted by the Supreme Court:

"However, it cannot be understood as laying a law that in every case of tortuous liability recourse must had to be a suit. When an infringement of Article 21 is apparent, it cannot be said that there will be any bar to proceed under Article 226 of the Constitution."[229]

Consequently, in *Rudal Sah* case, compensatory jurisprudence took a clear shape even though the framework was laid down in the *Khatri* judgment. Through the compensatory jurisprudence, the Supreme Court worded the right to life as a human right and offered the judicial administrators with an opportunity to provide victims with a glimmer of hope in the form of compensation in the light of wrongdoings & injustice heaped upon them by the State and its officers.

The Court in *Sebastian M. Hongray v. Union of India*[230] considered the case of two missing persons alleged to have been illegally kept under custody by the army and subsequently issued a writ of *habeas corpus*. The facts were such that two citizens were captured and died unnaturally in the custody of the military. In these situations, the Court kept in mind the torture, agony, and mental oppression undergone by the wives of the deceased and instead of imposing fine on the Government to the civil contempt of the Court, directed that:

"...as a measure of exemplary costs as is permissible in such cases, the Government should pay rupees one lakh to each one of the aforesaid two women."

The Supreme Court reiterated once again in the *Nilabati Behera alias Lalita Behera v State of Orissa*[231] that if State instruments or public servants violate basic rights, the Court could directly order the State to pay the victim or her heir, compensation through "monetary amends".

228 *Ibid.*

229 Jain, *supra* note 13 at 1535.

230 1984 AIR 571: 1984 SCR (1) 904: 1984 SCC (1) 339."

231 (1993) 2 SCC 746.

In such cases, the court held the '*sovereign immunity*' principle is not applicable.[232]

Smt. Nilabati Behera, alias Lalita Behera sent Supreme Court a letter in this case. This letter itself was treated as a writ petition under Article. 32 of the Constitution for determining the compensation demand made therein, arising from the death of the applicant's son, Suman Behera aged approximately 22 years in police custody.

It has been reported that in the morning of February 1, 1987, at approximately 8 a.m. Suman Behera was taken from his home, in association with an investigation of a robbery by Sarat Chandra Barik, Assistant Sub-Inspector, Bisra, District Sundergarh, Orissa and was detained. At approximately 2 p.m. on February 2, the petitioner came to know that her son, Suman's dead body was found from the Jaraikela railway station, on the distant track near a bridge. His body sustained several injuries, and it was clear that the death was unnatural, resulted due to those injuries.

The allegation was that he died in custody, and his body was subsequently thrown on the track. The petition demanded that applicant be given compensation for the violation of the basic right to life ensured by the Indian Constitution Article 21.

The respondent defended that Suman Behera had managed to escape from police custody at about 3 a.m. on the night between the 1st and 2nd December 1987 from the police outpost Jaraikela, where he was detained and guarded by police constable Chhabil Kujur. He was then unable to be arrested despite a search and on the railway line the next day he was found dead with several injuries, which proved that after he fled the police custody, he was run over by the passing train. The custodial death charge was therefore denied and consequently, the respondent's responsibility for his unnatural death.

In such a case, the District Judge prosecuted this matter in compliance with the court's instructions. Suman Behera died of several injuries caused to him, although he was detained at Jaraikela Police station, and the report's conclusions were based on evidence. However,

232 *Ibid.*

the report was considered to be disputed by the Court. Additional solicitor general relied on the respondent's defense that Suman had managed to escape from custody and was run over by a passing train when he sustained the fatal injuries. While a custodial death was found, the contention was that there was a lack of credible basis for exercise of such state obligations. But petitioner's amicus curiae, Shri M.S. Ganesh, argued that facts submitted at times of inquiry didn't help the respondents and there does not contain any explanation why the district judge had heard that Suman Behra had been already dead in police custody following wounds inflicted on him.

In *Nilabati Behera's* case it has been noted by the Supreme Court:

"It may be mentioned straight away that award of compensation in a proceeding under Article 32 by this Court or by the High Court covered by Article 226 of the Constitution is a remedy available in public law, based on strict liability for contravention of fundamental rights to which the principle of sovereign immunity does not apply, even though it may be available as a defence in private law in an action based on tort."[233]

It has been observed by Court that its enforcement power placed an obligation to create new instruments, the compensation of which was sufficient wherein it was only means to practicable redressal. It wasn't a misguided solution, however a public remedy; depending on rigorous liabilities for the infringement of fundamental rights that is not regulated by the sovereign immunity principle.

Furthermore, it has been emphasized by Anand J.:

"The state must ensure that there is no infringement of the indefeasible right of a citizen to life, except the following law while the citizen is in its custody. The precious right guaranteed by Article 21 of the Constitution of India cannot be denied to convicts, under trials, or other prisoners in custody, except according to the procedure established by law. There is a great responsibility on the police or prison authorities to ensure that the action in its custody is not deprived of his right to life. His liberty is in the very nature of things circumscribed by the very fact of his confinement and

233 *Supra* note 267 at 758

therefore his interest in the limited liberty left to him is rather precious. The duty of care on the part of the State is strict and admits of no exception."

The Supreme Court reiterated its stand taken from *Rudul Sah* in *M.C. Mehta v. Union of India*[234], that apart from issuing directions, it can forge new remedies under Article 32 and fashion new strategies designed to enforce the fundamental rights. The Court also claimed that, when the rights were violated, the power under Article 32 was not limited to preventive measures.[235] The court also noted that a conflicting situation would deprive Article 32 of its full usefulness and make it powerless and pointless.

The most significant point decided by the Bench decided was if Supreme Court could make statements for damages in constitutional rights violation as well as it has been observed that in appropriate circumstances, the Court still possess powers for awarding compensations wherein:

"The infringement of the fundamental right must be gross and patent, that is, incontrovertible and ex facie glaring & either such infringement should be on a large scale to affecting the fundamental rights of a large number of persons, or it should appear unjust or unduly harsh or oppressive on account of their poverty or disability or socially or economically disadvantaged position to require the person or persons affected by such infringement to initiate and pursue action in the civil courts."

In *Kanaka Rana v. State of Orissa*[236], the events & circumstances that gave rise to the case are quite interesting. The petitioner seemed to believe that she was a poor woman where her husband was a mechanic, who made a living with a truck and a workshop to fix others in Jaipur. After two baby girls, she & her husband agreed not to have a third child and opted for a family planning operation. In 1994, a medical officer conducted a tubectomy at Jaipur Road. Surprisingly, she gave birth to a female child in 2000. The petitioner's husband reported the matter to the various health & family welfare authorities and demanded damages, but no action was taken. A writ petition was filed,

234 "(1987) 1 SCC 395.

235 *Id.* at 405."

236 AIR 2009 Orissa 17

seeking compensation for conducting an unsuccessful tubectomy. In exceptional circumstances, despite a successful operation, a sterilized woman can sometimes become pregnant due to natural causes. In such cases, the best remedy available to her is to get the pregnancy terminated as it is permissible under the provisions of the Medical Termination of Pregnancy Act, 1971.

The Court observes further:

"The cause of action for claiming compensation in cases of failed sterilization operation arises on account of the negligence of the surgeon and not an account of childbirth. Failure due to natural causes would not afford any ground claim. It is for the girl who is conceived the child to go or not to go for medical termination of pregnancy. Having gathered the knowledge of conception despite having undergone the sterilization operation, if the couple opts to bearing the child, it ceases to be an unwanted child. Compensation for maintenance and upbringing of such child cannot be claimed."

The powers granted to Supreme Court in the Article 32, an important right itself, imposes a constitutional obligation on the Court to forge such new tools, which may be required for doing complete justice & enforcing fundamental rights guaranteed in the Constitution, which enable the award of monetary compensation in appropriate cases, where that is the only mode of redress available. The contrary view would not only the render the Court powerless but declare the Constitutional guarantee a mirage. However, it may, in certain situations, if for the extreme contraventions the Court is powerless to grant any relief against the State, except by punishment of the wrongdoers for the offense, and recovery of damages under private law, by the ordinary process. If the guarantee that deprivation of life & personal liberty cannot be made except under law is to be real, the enforcement of the right in case of every contravention must also be possible in the constitutional scheme, with appropriate mode of redress as per the facts of each case. This remedy in public law has to be made readily available when invoked by the disadvantaged, who are not possessed of the means for enforcement of their rights in private law, even though its exercise is to be toughened by judicial restraint to avoid circumvention of private law remedies.

In *S.P. Sampath Kumar v. Union of India*[237] on the ground that a legislative body can make efficient alternative institutional structures or legal review agreements without violating the Constitution's basic structure, the Court upheld Article 323-A which provides for an administrative tribunal with no discrimination to the jurisdiction any court except the Supreme Court.

In *Kihoto Hollohan v. Zachillhu*[238] the court invalidated para 7 of Constitution's 10th Schedule, as it amends the powers of High Court & the Supreme Court without following the procedure required in the proviso to Article 368(2). Although the tribunal was logical with the invalidity of para 7, the consequences of this disability on the remainder of the tenth schedule were split between 3 and 2.

While applying the *Doctrine of Severability*, the majority found, that para 7 was separable from the remainder of the Schedule & therefore did not affects its validity. Nevertheless, the minority held the opinion that first, para 7 could no longer be isolated from the remainder of the Schedule, and second, the doctrine of severability could not be used, even if it had been, to an amendment requiring the procedure observance, though not adherence, placed in the proviso to clause (2) of Article 368. The amendment was first invalidated for failure to comply with process provided for in Article 368, Clause (2).

In *Raghunathrao Ganpatrao v. Union of India*[239] the Supreme Court upheld Constitution (Twenty-sixth Amendment) Act, 1971 which derecognized the former Indian rulers and abolished their privy purses and other privileges by repealing Articles 291 and 362; and inserting Article 363-A. The Court observed that the repealed provisions were an integral part of the Constitution but didn't find them to constitute a basic structure of the Constitution. It rather found the amendment in consonance with republicanism, human dignity, and equality

237 (1987) 1 SCC 124: AIR 1987 SC 386

238 1992 Supp (2) SCC 651: AIR 1993 SC 412.

239 1994 Supp (1) SCC 191; AIR 1993 SC 1267."

proclaimed in the Preamble & running through the Constitutional provisions.

In *L. Chandra Kumar v. Union of India*[240], Supreme Court rules that its jurisdiction according to Article 32 as well as the high courts under Article 226 had been removed to the degree that Articles 323-A and 323-B were eliminated. The Court stressed that the judicial review was an integral characteristic of the Constitution which cannot be weakened by the transmission into administrative tribunals of judicial power and without the review of decisions according to Article 32 or 226. In this opinion consideration, as well as the availability under Court's Article 226 for judicial review against tribunals, the Court decided that if, after appointment by the High Court's Chief Justice, a retired Judge is selected for deliverance of Justice in consultation with High Court Chief Justice or a sitting Judge so appoints with the approval of the Chief Judge.

The *Vishaka v. State of Rajasthan*[241] Supreme Court held such that it is duty of the employer or other responsible person in the workplace and other institutions, whether public, private, to prevent sexual harassment of working women. Unless legislation has been enforced towards this end, the Apex Court provided a detailed guideline for stopping working women's sexual abuse in their workplaces.

The Court ruled it as:

"Sexual harassment includes such distasteful sexually determined behaviour as physical contacts and advances, showing pornography of sexual demands, whether by words or actions. Such conduct can be humiliating and constitute a health and safety problem, it is discriminatory when a woman has reasonable ground to believe that her refusal would disadvantage her in connection with her employment, including recruiting or promoting, or when it creates a hostile working environment. Remedies including compensation should be provided."

240 (1997) 3 SCC 261: AIR 1997 SC 1125
241 "(1997) 6 SCC 141: AIR 1997 SC 3011.

Therefore, in *Vishaka*, Chief Justice J.S. Verma speaking for Supreme Court clearly said that:[242]

"Gender equality includes protection against sexual harassment and right to work with dignity, which is a universally recognized basic human right. The common minimum requirement of this right has accepted global acceptance."

Chief Justice A.S. Anand observed in the *Apparel Export Promotion Council v. A.K. Chopra (Apparel Export Case)*[243]:

"There is no gainsaying that each incident of sexual harassment at the place of work, results in the violation of the fundamental right to gender equality and the right to life and liberty – the two most precious fundamental rights guaranteed by the Constitution of India."

The *I.R. Coelho v. the State of T.N.*[244] bench of nine judges, led by Sabharwal CJ, unanimously reaffirmed the law laid down in *Waman Rao*. It gave certain clarifications concerning the tests to be applied for judging the validity of amendments.

The Supreme Court in *Ashok Kumar v. Union of India*[245] upheld the validity of the Ninety-third Amendment of the Constitution which inserted clause (5) in Article 15 applicable to public educational institutions. The majority of four judges didn't test its application to private institutions because no such institution approached it. The dissenting single judge, however, invalidated it in so far as it applies to private unaided institutions.

R.A. Posner perceived "Judicial activism" as:

"...a view of the capacity and responsibility of courts relative to other agencies of government."[246]

The expansion of competence is advantageous in general and for the weaker parts of everyone's basic rights.

---

242 *Ibid.*
243 (1999) 1 SCC 759
244 (2007) 2 SCC 1.
245 (2008) 6 SCC 1."
246 Richard A. Posner, Overcoming Law 5 (Universal Law Publishing Co. Pvt. Ltd., New Delhi, 2007).

THE JUDGE'S CASE AND THE PARLIAMENT

Only an intact system can work. If there is a crack in that system, patchwork can never do. The same was the case with our judicial system.

Quoting Mehr Chand Mahajan:

"Nehru has always acted following the advice of the CJI."[247]

But issues rose when the system crashed, and unwritten standards were blurted. The judiciary that had eventually ruled the law constitutionally in compliance with Article 141 was in a difficult situation finding that the CJI had no primacy over the government's decision to nominate senior judges of the court. However, a decade later to that, the Supreme Court began fixing the damage and cure its injuries.[248] But, it went to a different extreme. The Constitution is well known to be supreme in our system, and it is a responsibility to respect all the institutions, including the judiciary.

Article 124 (2) provides for the appointment of the Supreme Court judges:

"Every Judge of the Supreme Court shall be appointed by the President by warrant under his hand & seal after consultation with such of the Judges of the Supreme Court & the High Courts in the States as the President may assume necessary for the purpose"

While for the High Court's judges, Article 217 (1) indicates:

"Every Judge of a High Court shall be appointed by the President by warrant under his hand & seal after consultation with the Chief Justice of India, the Government of the State, and, in the case of appointment of a Judge other than Chief Justice, the Chief Justice of the High Court."

247 Mehr Chand Mahajan, A Pillar of Justice quoted, "Granville Austin, Working A Democratic Constitution: A History of The Indian Experience 131 (Oxford University Press, New Delhi, 2006).

248 S.P. Gupta v. Union of India, AIR 1982 SC 149, 1981 Supp (1) SCC 87, 1982 2 SCR 365.

However, the court has invented a better procedure for such nominations, in the light of the fact that the Constitution has a clear selection mechanism for judges of the High Court & Supreme Court.

The question of immunity from public interest *(Crown Privilege's Indian law)* emerged in the *S.P. Gupta v. Union of India* (known as the Judges' case). In a circular issued by the union minister of Law on 18 March 1981 demanding that the Chief Minister inquire more judges at their state's High Court if they agree to their transfer as judged outside the state to the High Court; it was an appeal. No confirmation was granted to two of Delhi's three additional High Court judges. The government refused to place the correspondence claiming public immunity privilege but six of the seven judges, following *Conway v. Rimmer*, ordered the documents to be disclosed after examining them privately.

Justice Bhagwati strongly ruled that failure to reveal records would place the Government in an invincible position and would overwhelm any damage that could be caused by non-disclosure to the public interest. Furthermore, he determined that a failure to confirm an additional judge could only be questioned for two reasons:

That the Union Government was crystal clear from the debates to not hold absolute and successful consultations with the High Court's Chief Justice, the State Government as well as India Chief Justice, and

That the decision, not to confirm it was *mala fide*.

The Constitution is quite unambiguous as well as clear. In appointing a Supreme Court judge, *"the Chief Justice of India shall be consulted"*.

The President's power is not unfettered.

A bench of 9 judges heard the case of the *Supreme Court Advocates-on-Record Assn. v. Union of India*[249] (Second Judges Case). The Bench has added two novel concepts concerning the nomination of Superior Court judges, through majority decisions delivered by Verma J. (for himself, in support of Bharucha, Dr. Anand, Ray, and Dayal JJ).

249 AIR 1994 SC 868

Firstly, the CJI means not only the Chief Justice with absolute power of veto in the appointments, but collegiums; and

Secondly, the CJI shall have primacy in the decision of appointment over the President or the Executive of the day. In essence, the Supreme Court fortified judicial appointments.

Of course, there are also agreements such as appoint the senior most judge as the Chief Justice and raising the judges to the Supreme Court depending on their dominance at the High Court, which can be viewed as a positive trend. But it could not work without the practice of ensuring judicial independence.

The CJI overlooked most senior judges when nominating, which in Article 143 of the Constitution required the presidential reference. A nine-judge bench heard the reference. The court's opinion was presented by Bharucha J. The Court had to make its stance clearer.

Thus, in the *Second Judges' case*,[250] the court completely snatched the power of appointment and transfer of judges of the superior judiciary from the executive. It stipulated that the consultation provision for the CJI meant that he would be able to consent and hence gave power to collegium of judges including the CJI as well as two top judges. It has been extended to five: – CJI as well as four senior judges, for appointment to the Supreme Court, when it was referred to it by the President.

In the name of their independence and fully contrary to the constitutional scheme of founding fathers, this was an unfailing usurpation of authority by the judiciary. Some have correctly characterized the *Habeas Corpus* case as a precarious decision. In fact, the *Habeas Corpus* and *Second Judges'* cases are two poles between which the Supreme Court have moved with remarkable flexibility is perpetuating illegality. In the former, it cringed before the Executive in the name of express law, while in the latter; it went against the express provision and intentions of the Constitution makers which are crystal clear from debates & proceedings of the Constituent Assembly.

250 *Ibid.*

The new concept of collegiums evolved in the *Second Judges case*, was affirmed in the *Re Special Reference No. 1 of 1998*[251] (Third Judges case), however in the collegiums the judge's number has been increased.

Three have been three Judges cases—the first, decided by seven judges; the second, decided by nine judges; and the third, also decided by nine judges. Thus, in total twenty-five judges have applied their minds to the vital issues relating to judicial independence.

The present position is that the Chief Justice's view has primacy over the government's view. The President/government doesn't have power to veto; the proposed name can be remitted for reconsideration to the CJ/collegiums, but when returned and again proposed, the President/government cannot veto it.

In *Vinay Chandra Mishra, re*, Bar Council of India's Chairman, Mr. V.C. Mishra, faced contempt of court charges for:

"Obstructing the course of justice by trying to threaten, overawe & overbear the Court by using insulting, disrespectful and threatening language".

Mr. Mishra was angry at the question put to him by the S.K. Keshote J during a hearing of a court. Keshote J (junior judge on a bench) and began shouting, saying that he would get the judge transferred and see that an impeachment motion was brought against him in Parliament. Keshote J wrote to the acting Chief Justice of the High Court noting that such an incident was of concern to the whole system & not simply an insult to a judge. The acting Chief Justice of the High Court forwarded the letter to the Chief Justice of India who entertained it and constituted a three-judge Bench, consisting of K.N. Singh, Sawant, and Verma JJ. In the counter-affidavit, Mr. Mishra counter-charged Keshote J with committing contempt of his court. Meeting out the preliminary objections of Mr. Mishra, the Supreme Court found contemner guilty of committing criminal contempt of the court.

The Supreme Court, using its authority under Article 129 and 142, issued the order:

251 (1998) 7 SCC, 739: AIR 1999 SC 1.

"(a) the contemner Vinay Chandra Mishra is hereby sentenced to undergo simple imprisonment for a period of six weeks.

(b) The contemner shall stand suspended from practicing as an advocate for a period of three years from today."

The Supreme Court Bar Association brought a petition under Article 32 against the suspension order.[252] Taking into explanation the severity of the issue, a constitutional bench was set up on reference of the Division Bench. Both Kapil Sibal and Dr. Rajeev Dhavan argued that Supreme Court couldn't pass any order either under Article 142 or Article 129 to suspend a license of an advocate contemner, for which statutory provision otherwise exists (Advocates Act, 1961). The Supreme Court speaking through Anand J went on the back foot. The Court reported that:

"It, however, needs to be remember that the powers conferred on the Court by Article 142 being curative in nature cannot be construed as powers to authorize the Court to ignore the substantive rights of a litigant while dealing with a cause pending before it. This power cannot be used to 'supplant' substantive law applicable to the case or cause under consideration of the Court."[253]

There seems to be a great deal of doubt about the decisions, depending on a literal interpretation as well as restricting the interpretation of the term 'between the parties' as used in Article 142.

The contempt proceeding in *re, Vinay Chandra Mishra*, was initiated upon the initiative of Keshote J, in which there was a threat to the integrity of the court. He said:

"In case the dignity of the judiciary is not restored, then it is very difficult for the Judges to discharge their judicial function without fear or favour. Was not the Union of India standing for the court? It is submitted that taking a real and functional approach it was the court whose interest and dignity was involved, and Supreme Court refused to do justice to the judiciary on the technicality of an express statutory provision."[254]

---

252 Supreme Court Bar Association v. Union of India, (1998) 4 SCC 409, 431-32.

253 *Ibid.*

254 *Ibid.*

The Supreme Court itself identified the seriousness of the matter, and in that situation, judicial hands-off was not the suitable remedy for the vindication of the court's dignity, threatened by the mighty power that might be. It is an example where the judiciary exercises activism only to later go on the back foot.

Similarly, the Supreme Court overstepped its jurisdiction, and directed the government to create an all-India judicial service to bring about uniformity in the service conditions of judges of the subordinate judicial branch.[255]

Again, in another PIL, Supreme Court has given instructions for a substantial increase in its pay and benefits, which has contributed to serious financial pressures on the state government.[256]

Eight state governments filed an affidavit in the Court arguing that they couldn't bear such a significant burden on their exchequers. However, the Court rejected their pleas saying that financial crunch was no grounds for not implementing its directions. This is an apparent case of hindrance, as wages, benefits, and terms of service are subject matters of the government. Furthermore, the court is not concerned with the financial consequences but rather with philosophies, where the harsh financial realities are unignorable.

JUDICIAL ACTIVISM AND HUMAN RIGHTS JURISPRUDENCE

The backbone of human rights jurisprudence is illustrated by judicial activism. In the beautiful lines of *Rabindranath Tagore*, the process of transforming the non-beings into human beings is eloquently described:

"Into the mouths of these dumb, pale and weak,

We have to infuse the language of the soul,

Into the hearts of these weary and worn, dry and forlorn,

We have to minstrel the language of humanity."[257]

255 All India Judge's Association v. Union of India, (1992) 2 SCC 428

256 All India Judge's Association v. Union of India, (1998) 2 SCC 204.

257 Rao, *supra* note 176 at 21.

The word "Human Rights" is certainly a logical development of the 20th century. However, the concept of inalienable human rights is far older, with poets, philosophers, and politicians expressed this idea even in ancient times. Human rights are the genesis of the utopian idea of natural rights that can be traced from or even before the Greeks' control. Natural rights theory relies on a belief in 'Nature' as the primary force that gave each person the power to discover, for the sake of reason, the right principles to organize their lives. Natural rights also refer to any situations, circumstances, or actions that are right, rather than human neutral or wrong. For starters, if we have the inherent right to be free, being free is by default not a wrong.

The Magna Carta (1215), the Bill of Rights (1628), and the English Bill of Rights (1689) were proof of the increasing popular view that the human-beings were endowed with certain eternal and inalienable rights.

The findings by Justice Felix Frankfurter on an issue from the thirties, apply to the still emerging India of the 21st century:

"It is ideal to feel either the blind resentment against 'Government of Commission' or sterile longing for the golden past that never was. Profound new forces call for new social inventions or fresh adaptations of old experiences. The

'Great society' with its permeating influence of technology, large-scale industry, and progressive urbanization presses its problems; the history of political & social liberty admonishes us of its lessons. Nothing less is our task than the fashioning instruments and processes at once adequate for social needs and the protection of individual freedom."[258]

As stated by jurisprudence theory:

"A right is distinguished as positive or negative according to the nature of the correlative duty. In the case of a positive right, the person subject to duty

258 P.M. Bakshi, Public Interest Litigation 556 (Ashoka Law House, New Delhi, 3rd edn., 2012).

is bound to do something whereas, in case of a negative right, the person subject to duty is restrained from doing something."[259]

During the post-emergency times, the effects of judicial activism were negative as well as positive, where rights to achieve the preambular objectives of securing justice - economic, social, and political.

M.C. Mehta v. State of Tamil Nadu[260] was an instance where a Public Interest Litigation have been filed to highlight the condition of child labourers working in the match factories in Sivakasi in Tamil Nadu. As Professor Sathe pointed out, the Court felt that it should travel outside the boundaries of Sivakasi and discuss the issue as a national issue in a wider and broader perspective.[261]

The Court by the nature of its decision seems driven by the sociological jurisprudence and preferred social change in society. The Court refused to confine its role to a passive observer merely awaiting the efforts of the other two organs of the government to bring about social transformation visualized in the directive principles of the state policy. Instead, it proposed an active position to make social change visualized in state policy guidelines.

THE APEX COURT: A CRITIC OF ACTIVIST APPROACH OF JUDICIARY

For reminding the critics of the Judiciary's activist approach, the Supreme Court's outlook in *M.P. Oil Extraction v. K.N. Oil Industries.*[262] can be referred. The court explained:

"The supremacy of each of the three organs of the State, i.e., Legislature, Executive and Judiciary in their respective field of operation needs to be emphasized. The power of judicial review of the executive & legislative action must be kept within the bounds of the constitutional scheme so that there may not be any occasion to entertain misgivings about the rule of Judiciary in out-stepping its limit".

259 N. V. Paranjape, Studies In Jurisprudence And Legal Theory 237 (Central Law Agency, Allahabad, 2nd edn., 2007).

260 AIR 1997 SC 699: (1996) 6 SCC 756.

261 Sathe, *supra* note 21 at 242.

262 (1997) 7 SCC 592: AIR 1998 SC 145P: 1997 AIR SCW 4104.

In *State of U.P v. Johri Mal*, wherein the judicial review was further developed; Supreme Court placed down the following guidelines:

"The limited scope of judicial review, succinctly put, is:

1. *Courts, while exercising the power of judicial review, do not sit in appeal over the decisions of administrative bodies.*
2. *A petition for a judicial review will lie only on certain well-defined grounds.*
3. *An order passed by an administrative authority exercising discretion vested in it, cannot be interfered in a judicial review unless it is shown that exercise of discretion itself is perverse or illegal. A mere wrong decision beyond anything more is not enough to attract the power of judicial review; the supervisory jurisdiction conferred on a Court is limited to seeing to the tribunal functions within the limits of its authority & that its decisions do not occasion a miscarriage of justice.*
4. *The Court cannot be called upon to undertake the Government duties and functions. The Court is not to ordinarily interfere with a policy decision of the State. The social and economic belief of a judge should not be invoked as a substitute for the judgment of the legislative bodies."*[263]

It has been justified by Supreme Court that its restrictive political position in the above guidelines and rejected the pleading in *Binny Ltd. v. V. Sadasivan*[264] for the issuance of a writ of Mandamus.

Kuldip Nayar v. Union of India[265] also reveals the judiciary's attempt to legitimize Union law.

During the literal reading of Article 282 of the Indian Constitution, the Supreme Court's textual, legalist, and constructive approach, taken in the *Bearer Bonds case*[266] and *Habeas Corpus case*[267], prevailed while

263 *Supra* note 310.
264 AIR 2005 SC 3202: 2005 AIR SCW 3774: (2005) 6 SCC 657
265 (2006) 7 SCC 1: AIR 2006 SC 3127.
266 (1981) 4 SCC 675.
267 AIR 1976 SC 1207.

declaring the 'Member of Parliament Local and Area Development Scheme (MPLAD Scheme).'

Article 282 reads:

"The Union or a State will make any grants for any public purpose, notwithstanding that the purpose is not one concerning which Parliament or the Legislature of the State, as the case may be, may make laws."

In *Bhim Singh v. Union of India*[268] the MPLAD scheme's constitutionality was questioned.

The High Court in *Rajesh Maan v. Delhi Metro Rail Corporation*[269] restrained itself from exercising the power of judicial review on the issue of allotment of spaces of Metro station and license fee. The Court expressed its limitation by clarifying that it is a matter of State policy.

In *Ashwini Kumar Chopra v. Union of India*[270], the same view is reiterated by the same Court to avoid interfering between the State districts regarding the dam water distribution.

The Supreme Court in *Kachchh Jal Sankat Nivaran Samiti v. State of Gujarat*[271] held that there must be judicial restraint in such matters, like the above cases & the case of *Divisional Manager, Aravali Golf Club v. Chander Hass.*[272]

In *Union of India v. Dr. Kushala Shetty*[273], the Supreme Court of India has reaffirmed that judicial inquiries have restricted scope and that their powers of judicial reviews are still limited as the Judiciary is founded on Constitutional wisdom.

The Supreme Court applied method in its judgment in *Grid Co. Ltd. v. Sadananda Doloi*[274]. The beauty of the decision lies in the Court's rationale approach, which says:

---

268 (2010) 5 SCC 538

269 AIR 2010 Del 396 (NOC)

270 AIR 2011 Del 154.

271 AIR 2011 SC 2747: 2011 AIR SCW 4336: (2011) 8 SCALE 26.

272 (2008) 1 SCC 683: AIR 2008 SC (Supp) 360: 2008 AIR SCW 406.

273 AIR 2011 SC 3210: 2011 AIR SCW 4460: (2011) 7 SCALE 654.

274 AIR 2012 SC 729.

"It cannot sit in the armchair of the Administrator to decide whether a more reasonable decision or course of action could have been taken in the circumstances. So long as the action taken by an authority is not shown to be vitiated by the infirmities referred to above and so long as the action is not demonstrably in outrageous defiance of logic, the writ Court would do well to respect the decision under challenge."

As regards the importance of a written constitution which also contains *judicial review*, Chief Justice of India, Hon'ble Mr. K.G. Balakrishnan cited Justice Aharon Barak's remark:[275]

"To maintain real democracy and to ensure a delicate balance among its elements – a formal constitution is preferable. To operate effectively, a constitution should enjoy normative supremacy, should not be as easily amendable as a normal statute, & should give judges the power to review the constitutionality of legislation. Without a formal constitution, there is no legal limitation on legislative supremacy, and the supremacy of human rights exists only by the grace of the majority's self-restraint. A constitution, however, imposes legal limitations on the legislature and guarantees that those human rights are protected not only by the self-restraint of the majority but also by constitutional control over the majority. Hence, the need for a formal Constitution."

JUDICIARY: THE COUNTER MEASURE OF LEGISLATURE INITIATIVE

The constitutional framers had a simple vision: they gave the courts prestige but decided to coordinate their status based on collaboration along with the two other government branches. The powers of review of the judiciary were very limited in terms of the right to property and personal rights. Pandit Jawaharlal Nehru felt the same. He said:

"Within limits, no judge and no Supreme Court make itself a third chamber [of the legislature]. No Supreme Court and no judiciary can stand in judgment over sovereign will of Parliament representing the will of the entire community. If we go wrong here and there, it can point it out, but in the ultimate analysis, where the future of the community is concerned; no

275 Hon'ble Mr. K.G. Balakrishnan, Judicial Activism Under Indian Constitution (Address at Trinity College Dublin, Ireland – October 14, 2009)

judiciary can come in the way. And if it comes in the way, ultimately the whole Constitution is a creature of Parliament."[276]

Sardar V.B. Patel was again concerned with the position of conservative judges. His weariness showed that:

"There is a danger that certain old type of Judges may misinterpret this new process of law."[277]

The Supreme Court again started with a minimal approach. The Supreme Court has adopted a positive/restraint approach in *A.K. Gopalan v. State of Madras*[278] (Gopalan).

In *Golak Nath v. State of Punjab*, wherein the Constitution's 1st, 4th, and 17th Amendment Acts were declared illegal, had a significant negative position.[279]

In *Kesavananda Bharati v. the State of Kerala*[280], the Parliament made numerous amendments, e.g., 24th and 25th, to annul the consequences of judicial decisions upheld in the judgment.

The scope of the post-emergency property rights is not quite distinct from the earlier one, in view of *Maneka Gandhi v. Union of India*[281], 'just, fair and reasonable' requirement has become the test based on which the validity of a law under which property is acquired shall be determined.

The Supreme Court's decision in *Kerala v. Peoples Union for Civil Liberties*[282] showed that, regardless of the intent of the legislative act, the jurisprudence on compensation evolved by the Court within the first decade was still the same.

Once upon a time education was a reverent way of illumination with scientific temper.

---

276 C. A. D. (Vol. IX) 1195.

277 B. Shiva Rao, Proceedings of the Advisory Committee Meeting, Select Documents, Vol. II.

278 AIR 1950 SC 27: 1950 SCR 88.

279 AIR 1967 SC 1643: (1967) 2 SCR 762."

280 (1973) 4 "SCC 225: AIR 1973 SC 1461.

281 (1978) 1 "SCC 248: AIR 1978 SC 597."

282 (2009) 8 SCC 46.

Although, with added dimension that the right to a job is the part of constitution's fundamental framework, undermines social legitimacy, and extends the judicial control on the right to education. The judicial expansion of the right to education, is further granting consequential rights to establish educational institutions and conversion of education into a right to occupation of the unaided educational institution.[283]

THE APEX COURT'S RISING GLORY

The fall in the profile of politicians is an explanation of why the judges have a higher profile and the consequent credibility of the Court. The politicians were very influential and highly regarded during the Nehru rule. Some had suffered when fighting for independence and they gained reputation from the glory of sacrifice. On the other hand, the Judges have been appointed by the colonial government and considered mere technocrats. Nehru himself had an exceedingly limited view of the Judges & the legal proceedings. He assumed they would serve simply as arbiters to settle on the predetermined rules of the game. Also, a status quo image was provided by the judgments in favour of government. Over the years, however, the image of the politicians suffered, primarily because of a lack of ideological commitment and a tendency to use power for personal glorification. The 1975 emergency was a watershed, and after the Court's activism, the balance between judges and politicians was shifted. In the world, a feeling where judges are better guardians of the rights of people than the chosen legislative representative seem to have grown.[284]

In the name of the rule of law, the High Courts & the Supreme Court have begun to question some government decisions.

The question of the abuse of power in the allotment of petrol pumps was raised in *Common Cause v. Union of India*[285] (Petroleum Pump Case I), while arbitrary house allocations were raised in *Shiv Sagar Tiwari v. India*[286]. The Court went to the extent of slapping exorbitant fines of Rs. 50 lakhs and Rs. 60 lakhs on Satish Sharma and Sheila Kaul

283 Ashoka Kumar Thakur v. Union of India, (2008) 6 SCC 1;

284 Sathe, *supra* note 21.

285 "(1996) 6 SCC 530

286 (1996) 6 SCC 599.

respectively, the then Union ministers of the concerned departments. The Court again orders the Central Bureau of Investigation (CBI) to report on the matter regarding the arbitrary and unfaithful action of Captain Sharma in respect of a criminal breach of trust or other offense under the law. The Court had clarified that it was entitled, under its writ jurisdiction, as well as under the principles of public law, to impose damages for malfeasance.

In the *Jain Hawala case*[287], the Supreme Court ordered CBI to investigate impartially and report specifically on payments rendered to many politicians based on entries in Jain's journals. The court monitored the investigations conducted by the CBI and clarified that it had done so only because the superior authorities to whom the investigating officers were to report were themselves suspects & that the monitoring was to continue only till the filing of the charge sheet. Due to judicial activism, corruption has been exposed in high offices and penal action has been initiated against politicians and public servants. The hawala diaries would have gathered dust in the archives of the CBI if the Supreme Court has not forced the agents to act against the recipients of illegal money. The CBI was then urged by the Supreme Court to press on the matter. On 1 March 1996, the Court directed to the CBI not to report to higher administrative bodies, including the Prime Minister, the progress in hawala scam investigations.

The Court provided similar instructions for monitoring in the *Fodder Scam case* in Bihar. *Vineet Narain v. Union of India*[288] (1998) showed how to structure the CBI to be resistant to external pressures and how to choose its chief:

"The establishment and working of investigation agencies revealed the lacuna of its inability to perform whenever powerful persons were involved. For this reason, a close examination of the establishment of these agencies & their control assumes significance. No doubt, the overall control of the agencies and responsibility of their functioning must be in the executive,

287 Vineet Narain v. Union of India, (1996) 2 SCC 199: JT 1996 (1) 708.
288 "(1998) 1 SCC 226: AIR 1998 SC 889.

but then a scheme giving needed insulation from extraneous influences even of the controlling executive is imperative."[289]

This laid-back approach by the Executive and that of the legislature has been justified by the Supreme Court:

"The Executive must fill the vacuum by executive order because it is the field which is coextensive with that of the legislature & where there is inaction even by the executive, for whatever reason, the judiciary must step in, in the exercise of its Constitutional obligations under the aforesaid provisions [Article 32 and Article 142 of the Constitution] to provide a solution till the legislature acts to perform its role by enacting proper legislation to cover the field."[290]

The Supreme Court has created a third category, 'lifetime jail', in *Swami Shraddhananda @ Murali Manohar Mishra v. State of Karnataka*[291]. The Court noticed that the crime, in this case, was only below the "rarest" level, but life imprisonment, meaning 14 years in jail, was insufficient in view of the horrendous crime.

Through, *Ram Jethmalani & Others v. Union of India*[292] the issue of black money rocked the country that Indians spirited away anything between $500 billion and $1.5 trillion outside the country and deposited it at Swiss and Liechtenstein-based banks, before the 2009 Lok Sabha election. The BJP agreed to bring back the money if voted to power.

This dilemma has triggered a storm by the end of 2010. Subhash C. Kashyap et al[293] including Ram Jethmalani filed a PIL in the Supreme Court. The entire scandal about black money, surfaced that Hasan Ali Khan, a Pune-based stud farm owner, had allegedly stashed away $8 billion in Swiss banks. The Court frowned upon why no action was taken against Khan by the government.[294]

---

289 (1998) 1 SSC 243

290 *Ibid.*

291 AIR SC 2008 3040: (2008) 11 SCR 93."

292 Writ Petition (Civil) No(s). 176 of 2009 with SLP (C) no. 11032 of 2009.

293 *Ibid.*

294 Editorial, What the hell is going on: SC on Hasan Ali, The Times of India, New Delhi, 4 March 2011; Editorial, Why Govt. is soft on

Khan was arrested by the ED on 7 March 2011, following clear verbal observations by the Court. Hasan Ali obtained bail from Mumbai City Court after four days of his detention. But on 17 March, in an extraordinary move, the Supreme Court accepted a special leave plea directly contrary to the order of the district court, revoked Khan's bail, and sent him to judicial custody for four days.[295]

Finally, on 4 July 2011, the Supreme Court set up a Special Investigation Team (SIT) with Justices B.P. Jeevan Reddy and M.B. Shah as the chairman and the vice-chairman to probe the black money. It was for the first time that the Court took over an investigation by appointing a former judge of the Court as the chairman of the SIT.

The Supreme Court, after over 13 years, by taking an activist stance, quashed the appointment of P.J. Thomas as the CVC, in *Center for PIL & Anr v. Union of India & Anr*[296]. rejecting the Union Government's claim that it is the government's prerogative to nominate anybody. No court has ever set aside the appointment for such a high functionary before. The High-Powered Committee (HPC) re-emphasized Thomas' name for the CVC on 3 September 2010. The HPC included the Prime Minister, the Home Secretary, and the opposition leader. Opposition Leader Sushma Swaraj declared her dissent that Thomas was not fit to head the watchdog against corruption, as he was accused of illegally importing Palmolein. The Government dismissed the opposition & suggested the name of Thomas to the Chairman. The court while declaring the recommendation of the government to appoint Thomas 'non-est in law', stressed on transparency and the integrity of the decision-making process.

Again, Supreme Court ordered those investigations into the 2G Spectrum Scam would be done under its monitoring.[297] The Court directed that CBI would conduct a thorough investigation into various

---

Hasan Ali, asks SC, The Indian Express, New Delhi, 4 March 2011.

295 Assistant Director, Directorate of Enforcement v. Hasan Ali Khan, Petition for Special Leave to Appeal (Crl) No. 22455/2011

296 (2011) 4 SSC 1.

297 Centre for Public Interest Litigation & Others v. Union of India & Others, (2011) 1 SCC 560: 2010 (13) SCALE 501: 2010 INDLAW SC 1086.

issues highlighted in the report of the CVC (which was forwarded to the Director, CBI) and the report of the Comptroller and Auditor-General (CAG), who prima facie found serious irregularities in the grant of licenses to 122 applicants, majority of whom are said to be ineligible, the blatant violations of the terms and conditions of licenses and a huge loss to the exchequer running into several thousand crores. On 2 February 2012, the division bench of the Supreme Court, comprising Justices G.S. Singhvi and A.K. Ganguly, cancelled all 122, 2G licenses granted after 10 January 2008 during the tenure of A. Raja, declaring it as 'illegal'. Indicating A. Raja, Court directed that the licenses in 22 circles be sold by auction, and with fresh recommendations being made by the Telecom Regulatory Authority of India (TRAI).

It is hyperbolic and vulnerable to test that the judiciary is the most diligent guardian of liberty, democratic principles, and constitutionalism. The judiciary has itself encroached on the domain of others, disregarding the doctrine of separation of powers which itself goes against the spirit of democracy. Further, this reasoning is flawed in the sense that, the judiciary is the only institution that is sensitive and redresses the grievances of people who would have taken to the streets. If we accept that it is acting as the safety valve, how do we explain the mass unrest in the form of Naxalism – where Naxalites have their parallel courts – extremism and even terrorism in several parts of the country? The delay of the legislature & the executive body, however, is no less appalling, as the issue of judicial delays drives citizens to recourse to extra-constitutional instruments.

In *Nandini Sundar*[298] the Supreme Court announced the appointment of Special Police Officers (SPOs) unconstitutional which has been done under Sections 9 and 23 of the Chhattisgarh Police Act, 2007. The facts & situations which led to the appointments of the SPOs in Chhattisgarh were questioned. In Chhattisgarh, the Maoist/ Naxal violence had increased. To encounter and resist such activities, an organization named *Salwa Judum* started in 2006 to operate in rural areas. Both the opposition & the ruling parties were bipartisan in this campaign. The Chhattisgarh government subsequently adopted

298 (2011) 7 SCC 547: (2011) 2 SCC (L&C) 762

Salwa Judum and named SPOs and *Koya* commandos for the *Salwa Judum* organization. Maoist operations were distributed across the neighbouring states of Chhattisgarh, such as Jharkhand, Orissa, Andhra Pradesh, Maharashtra, Bihar, and U.P. And of course, and W.B. In 2009 the Central Government announced a proposal to co-ordinate counteroperations in countries affected by the Naxal Hit. *Salwa Judum* began a high-level anti-Naxal mission but later became more militant and unregulated. *Salwa Judum* had to be dissolved.

Salwa Judum was replaced by the SPOs. The government of Chhattisgarh had recruited SPOs to fight 'naxalitarian' terrorism under the Chhattisgarh Police Act of 2007. In the past, such SPOs had, according to Section 17 of the Police Act, 1861 been designated by a District Magistrate. Appointees from Chhattisgarh earned Rs. 3000, 80% of which was contributed by the Government of India each month.

In the *Nandini Sundar case* on 5 July 2011, the much-discussed Supreme Court ruled outlawing *Salwa Judum* and dissolving SPOs. This case came from a written petition from Dr. Nandini Sundar, 2) Dr. Ram Chandra Guha and 3) E.A.S. Sarma, filed in 2007. The key claim in this petition was that residents of Dantewada and neighbouring areas were widely violated. The government allegedly promoted the activities of *Salwa Judum*, an armed vigilant rebellion party. A further connection to this was the fresh allegation that, while on his way with other visitors to villages, Swami Agnivesh, a famous social worker, was allegedly attacked by members of *Salwa Judum* to provide humanitarian assistance to victims of the conflict.

The Court tried elsewhere to recognize & address the issue of Maoist terrorist activities. The Court considered problem to be solved by meeting the socio-economic expectations of the people through constitutional developments. The court stressed on the breach of human rights of young people working as SPOs on low pay without proper protection. It also found a complete infringement under Article 21 of the Constitution of the right to personal freedom.

The orders are issued by Supreme Court that:

1. Chhattisgarh shall cease to use the SPOs in all ways in all operations without unnecessary delay.
2. The Government of the Union shall refrain against making any findings for recruiting the SPOs.
3. 3. All firearms issued to SPOs shall be recalled by the government.
4. The Government of the State shall make the required security arrangements in the State.
5. The government shall take steps to prevent the operation of groups and investigate or file FIR against them. *viz Salwa Judum* and *Koya* commandos.

It was also clear that, while the State policies to fight terrorism and extremism are being affected, the judicial policy should not attempt to interfere with the safety consideration that is beyond the purview of the executive and legislature. The Bench was itself conscious of the effect of such decisions on executive policy. It intervenes only to implement constitutional principles and priorities.[299]

In *A Parent of a Student of Medical College, Shimla v. The State of HP*[300], the Supreme Court reversed the decision of the High Court and ordered the government to enact a law to curb college ragging. The Court ruled that High Court didn't have the power to give such a direction as it fell within the purview of the legislature. The Court decided that it was not qualified.

It was followed in *Asif Hameed v. State of Jammu & Kashmir.*"[301] The High Court rejected the orders of the state administration to make a statutory admittance committee by the Supreme Court. Once again, The Supreme Court ruled that the government cannot create posts for the tractor drivers.

A nine-judge Constitution Bench in *S.R. Bommai v. Union of India*, with a six-member majority, ruled that presidential satisfaction for dismissal of state governments is subject to judicial review.

299 *Id*, at 583-84, paras 81-82.
300 (1985) 3 SCC 169.
301 AIR 1989 SC 1899

In 2006, the dissolution of the Bihar Assembly was declared illegal.[302]

The Supreme Court ruled that even the decisions of the President & Governors were subject to judicial review in cases of forgiveness for convicts sentenced to death.[303]

Some decisions of the Supreme Court in the name of upholding the rule of law and the independence of the judiciary breach the boundary line, usurping the role assigned to others. Therefore, the Supreme Court provide guidelines that have the force of law. It laid down values and norms in the adoption of Indian children by foreigners. And the procedure to be followed for allowing passive euthanasia. In *Vishaka and Others v. State of Rajasthan.*[304] It issued orders to end the sexual abuse of women in the workplace & laid down its legal standards until an Act hadn't been passed by Parliament.

Likewise, in *D.K. Basu v. State of West Bengal*[305], detailed guidelines for the making of arrests and the concept of arrest rights including the right against torture were provided by the Supreme Court. It was a welcome decision because it was important to control the police barbarism. Furthermore, it ruled that the Executive should fill it if there is a legislative vacuum, otherwise the judiciary would do.

It also provided seven broad directions, one for Union and six for the states, for the fixed tenures for police officers and establishment of security committees at the state and central level, among others for police reforms.[306] In the interest of preserving the rule of law, it did so. It is true that police officers are also transferred for political purposes and many times shield criminals or hoodlums close to the powers that

302 Rameshwar Prasad & Others (VI) v. Union of India & Anr., (2006) 2 SCC 1.

303 Kehar Singh & Anr. V. Union of India & Anr., AIR 1989 SC 653: 1`989 Cri LJ 941: JT 1988 (4) SC 693: 1988 (2) SCALE 1965: (1989) 1 SCC 204.

304 AIR 1997 SC 3011: JT 1997 (7) SC 384: 1997 (5) SCALE 453: (1997) 6 SCC 241

305 (1997) 1 SCC 416: 1997 SCC (Cri) 92: AIR 1997 SC 610

306 Union of India v. Prakash Singh & Others, JT 2006 (12) SC 225: 2006 (9) SCALE 444: (2006) 8 SCC 1

are likely to be prosecuted. Several police commissions and the law commission made such recommendations, but it does not give the apex court a carte blanche to issue directions to give police officials fixed tenures. It also gave detailed guidelines for the selection of the CVC.[307]

The post-Kesavananda Bharti period was not a very happy one. The Executive passed orders resulting in three Supreme Court judges being superseded; judges of the High Court who decided habeas corpus cases in favour of the detenus were either being transferred, or their names were being leaked.

In *Sarla Mudgal v. Union of India*[308] (Sarla Mudgal), The Supreme Court consisting of K. Singh and R.M. Sahai JJ made a very appreciable attempt to vitalize the efforts to develop and enact a uniform civil law. The learned judge desired that Article 44 be retrieved from "the cold storage where it has been located since 1949."[309]

The row caused by the judicial review, Lord Woolf considered, is beneficial & appropriate for the rule of law to apply, and this uncertainty generated by the judicial review is reasonable because it demonstrates the role of the courts to ensure that day-to-day acts are taken in line with the law. The friction is a required product of preserving the balance that our constitution has to do with the Legislature, the executive, and the courts.[310]

Sometimes, even the government also assists with judicial review or opinions when it does not want to take a controversial decision. The Indian Constitutions (Article 143) and Canada (Supreme Court Act, 1875) state that, as a consulting judgment which is not binding, but which has important persuasive value, the government can refence of any matter of primary public interest to the Supreme Court. In India,

307 Centre for PIL & Anr. v. Union of India & Anr., (2011) 4 SCC 1.
308 (1995) 3 SCC 635: AIR 1995 SC 1531.
309 *Ibid* at 69
310 Lord Woolf, Judicial Review: The Tension among the Executive & the Judiciary, Christopher Campbell-Holt (Ed.), The Pursuit of Justice 133 (Oxford University Press, 2008).

The Ayodhya complication eluded the decision, and the government sent the issue back to the Supreme Court.

FINDINGS

It is quite evident that, under the Constitutional Scheme that allows the judiciary to play an active role in India and the Supreme Court, has extensive control.

In the security and promotion of human rights in India, the Supreme Court played a role as a saviour. The rule of the Court ensures that the promise of the nation to globally uphold human rights does not remain solely on paper.

Where it was considered vague in the Constitution to mention such rights, the Court through its dynamic interpretation mentioned the unenumerated human rights with the framework of Article 21 of the Constitution. Where the legislature was sluggish in dealing with core issues of human rights, until Parliament passed legislation on them, the Court developed guidelines to deal with these fundamental issues.

The time-tested solution is the power to grant a writ of mandamus to the relevant public authority to command the execution of its legal duty in the event of Government or administrative failures. However, a strong difference exists between the administrative role of this public body and the judicial authority itself. The former, and not the latter, is legitimate judicial intervention.

10. JUDICIAL ACTIVISM AND THE INDIAN CONSTITUTION

Judicial activism even though comparable to legislative activism, treads a dissimilar path. There are two types of legislative activism: activist law-making and dynamic law-making. Activist law-making allows the legislature to draw ideas from the current consensus that society maintains. Dynamic law-making means that the legislature generates proposals beyond the consensus and spreads them long before they are formulated. Dynamic law-making is legitimate as it is the establishment of legislators who have a common mandate themselves.

On the contrary, it is difficult for the Judges to assume the dynamic role of the legislators. Any idea which is alien to constitutional objectives cannot be transformed into a binding constitutional principle by judicial interpretation. The courts may, however, draw lines primarily from a new viewpoint by introducing creative processes, without resorting to a specific preference that leads towards that option (inviting criticization to the constitutionally forbidden field of judicial activism). The resulting circumstance may bring the credit or often prove detrimental to the judicial institution.

The claim that the widening horizon of judicial review has incorporated social and economic justice values, cannot be exaggerated. The field of public interest law or PIL (public interest litigation) as it is known in India is one in which the judiciary won the accolade, where the concept of *locus standi*[311] has been demonstrated to provide social justice for vast masses of people.

The meaning of the word 'litigation' (a judicial action that includes all proceedings in the case), initiated to impose a right or to seek redress.

Thus, lexically 'PIL' means Judicial action taken by the Court of Law for the implementation of the public interest or the general interest which involves a pecuniary interest in the public or any class of the society or which affects its juridical rights or obligations.

311 *Supra* note 176

'Public interest' means an act that is advantageous to the public in general. It refers to acts that are required for public purposes. The goal is to make justice accessible to the poor masses.[312] The origin of judicial activism is also said to be found in PIL's evolution and the consequent liberalization of the locus standi law.

The Supreme Court in 1979 first took a PIL in *Hussainara Khatoon v. the State of Bihar*,[313] on behalf of prisoners awaiting trial, who languished in jail for a period longer than the maximal sentence for that crime. The Court provided orders to ensure the prisoners were adequately relieved.

Judicial activism and PIL (Public interest litigation) go hand in hand. The result of judicial activism is the PIL itself. Under Article 32, in private matters and PIL in cases of breaches of basic rights can be brought directly before the Supreme Court. There are no criteria to judge the legitimacy of the activist approach taken by the Supreme Court, but the fact that disagreement has often rung from many quarters seems fair to comment. An independent study is needed to assess and evaluate the legitimization of PIL activism in the country.

LOCUS STANDI: THE CONCEPT

The right of a party to appear before any court or tribunal or be heard on a specific matter is *locus standi*. The Public Interest litigation originates from the Supreme Court's liberalization of *locus standi*. For public interest litigation to occur, someone else must be able to approach the court on behalf of others who cannot come by themselves, and that person need not be a 'person aggrieved' in the traditional sense.

'Locus Standi' as defined, in Black's Law Dictionary:

"It is the right to bring an action or to be heard in a given forum"[314]

312 Babu Ram Verma v. State of Uttar Pradesh, (1971) All LJ 653; (1971) Serv LR 649: (1971) 2 Lab LJ 235: (1971) Lab IC 162 (All).

313 AIR 1979 SC 1360: Cr LJ 1036: (1980) 1SCC 81".

314 Bryan A. Garner, Black's Law Dictionary 952 (West Thomson Reuters, 7th edn., 1999).

In the case of *People's Union for Democratic Rights v. Union of India*[315] while addressing the issue of *locus standi*, the Supreme Court considered the illiteracy, poverty, the ignorance obstructing and impeding accessibility of the judicial process, and the procedure, which led for the writ petition to be filed.

The party aggrieved by any order is usually entitled to obtain relief by bringing into question its validity, correctness, and legality. An individual who lodges a petition for an invocation of a basic right should have a direct or indirect interest in the result of that right, for themselves, or on behalf of a disabled person (therefore, for obvious purposes, it could not access the justice system without meeting any of the mentioned requisites.) There have been instances in which a publicly inspired person in *bona fide*, has sued for violations of fundamental rights, particularly in *habeas corpus* petitions. Also, in these cases, however, the participant must accept some observable relationship/ interest to the participating individuals, personally or to the public at large in case of a PIL. In these cases, the petitioner must demonstrate *bona fide*, by the truthful and cautious exercise of such right.[316]

Locus standi refers to the legal right one can claim to invoke the court's jurisdiction. When the petitioner has no locus standi, a Court of Law[317] does not hear him. The traditional look about the writ jurisdiction of locus standi has been that only such an individual has *locus standi* where –

1. a breach of his legal right or constitutionally protective interest has caused the legal injury; or
2. A legal injury is possibly due to a breach of his legal right or legally protected interest.

Thus, a person must have a personal or private right that is breached or threatened to be violated to obtain locus Standi. In the sense that

315 "AIR 1982 SC 1473: (1982) 2 SCC 494: (1982) 2 SCWR 202".

316 Kishore Samrite v. State of Uttar Pradesh, (2013) 2 SCC 398 (para 52).

317 Charan Lal Sahu v. Giani Zail Singh, (1984) 1 SCC 390: AIR 1984 SC 309: 1984 UJ (SC) 873.

he has suffered or is likely to suffer any discrimination, financial or otherwise, he should be 'person aggrieved'.[318]

The theory that, remedies, as well as rights, are correlative is common for the conventional concepts of *locus standi*. Thus, only a person whose right is at risk has the right to pursue a remedy.

These propositions of law are derived from this rule:

1. Just anyone who's personal or property rights have been specifically and significantly injured can take recourse to jurisdiction.
2. When an individual is subject to certain administrative actions with other members of the public, only if he can prove himself those specific injuries over and above what others have suffered, he can contest the action in question.
3. Where the person challenging an administrative action is a total stranger (courts call them meddlesome interloper), the court ordinarily does not entertain such a petition.[319]

PRO BONO PUBLIC (FOR THE GOOD OF THE PUBLIC)

In *pro bono* proceedings, courts may interfere when:

1. to restrain exploitation of labour practices
2. protection required for homes and persons or inmates
3. a lack of probity in public life and destruction of the environment
4. display of callous neglect in a state policy; and
5. abuse of power by those in control.

THE JOURNEY FROM DOCTRINE OR LOCUS STANDI TO PUBLIC INTEREST LITIGATION

One very critical method for the courts to prevent fraudulent or vicarious prosecutions is by making sure that the individual approaching the Court is in a condition to do so. This person must establish that his/

318 Adi Pherozshah Gandhi v. H.M. Seervai, (1970) 2 SCC 484: AIR 1971 SC 385: (1971) 1 SCR".

319 Jasbhai Motibhai Desai v. Roshan Kumar, (1976) 1 SCC 671.

her right has been explicitly abused and he/she is adversely harmed by the impugned act.

As stated by conventional rules, *locus standi* is the judicial redress available only to a person:

- Who has suffered a legal injury by means of a violation of his legal right or legally protected interest by the impugned action of the State/public authority/or any other person.
- Who is *likely to suffer* a legal injury by means of a threatened violation of his legal right or legally protected interest by any such action.

The qualitative twist of the Court concerning the conventional law of *locus standi* has, however, opened the door to PIL.

Where a legal wrong or injury is caused to a person by violation of any Constitutional or legal right and such person or a determinate class of person is on account of poverty, helplessness, disability, socially or economically disadvantaged position, unable to approach the Court for relief, then any member of the public can put up an application in the High Court for appropriate direction, order or writ (under Article 226 of the Constitution). Further, for the violation of any Fundamental Right of such person or determinate class of person, the remedy lies in the Supreme Court under Article 32 for seeking judicial redress for the legal wrong or injury.

The right to move the Supreme Court by appropriate proceedings for the enforcement of the fundamental rights is provided in Article 32(1). According to Article 32(2), the Supreme Court has the power to assess any proceedings for the protection of fundamental rights and to evaluate any process needed in a specific case. The remedial assistance which may even require to pay compensation in 'appropriate cases' may also be given by the Supreme Court in accordance with this Constitutional clause.

The liberal approach of *locus standi* allows PIL to be made by persons or organizations, against violation of human rights, in support of the economic exploitation, social tyranny, or political oppression of the victims.

Writ jurisdiction was meant to be exercised only for preventing mischief, not for providing relief for the mischief already done. When a man was arrested unlawfully, he will be set free by a judge, but could not render the wrongdoer compensable for his misdemeanour. The individuals affected had to prosecute or sue the police or any other authority responsible for such illegal detention.

After analysing several propositions, in India, it is assumed that the *locus standi* related laws depend on the following:

1. Class action suits may be started by any member of the class that is affected.
2. PIL, i.e., when an individual starts a proceeding not to enforce his personal but general or public social interests or a portion thereof.
3. Statutory standing, i.e., where statutes confer standing on an association as persons who have no personal standing in the matter, for example, trade unions, etc., as well as
4. Individual standing.[320]

The doctrine of *action populares* in Ancient Rome allowed any individual to bring an action in respect of public delict, but most of the common-law and civil-law systems today exclude such *action popularis* and require the applicant to show some sort of a direct and personal interest in the subject-matter of litigation before permitting him to maintain that action.

In *Ex parte Sidebotham*, James LJ constricted the meaning of the word *"person aggrieved"*, and he held that:

"The applicant must be a man against whom a decision has been pronounced which has wrongfully deprived him of something or wrongfully refused him something or wrongfully affected his title to something".[321]

320 M.A. Fazal, Judicial Control of Administrative Action In India, Pakistan And Bangladesh: A Comparative Study 77 (Butterworths India, New Delhi,3rd edn., 2000").

321 (1880) LR 14 Ch D 458.

The definition lasted nearly three-quarters of a century before in *Attorney General of Gambia v. N' Ji'* Lord Denning dismissed it and stated:

> *"The phrase 'person aggrieved' is of wide meaning and should not be subjected to a restrictive interpretation. They do not include, of course, a mere busy-body ... but they do include a person who has a genuine grievance because an order has been made that prejudicially affects his interests".*[322]

In *Regina v. Liverpool Taxi Owners' Assn., re,*[323] the association of taxi license holdings was given the standing to obtain prohibition to restrain the implementation of an order to increase the number of licenses without first hearing representations on behalf of interested persons.

In *Attorney General Ex rel. Mcwhirter v. Independent Broadcasting Authority,*[324] a civic member lodged an action for an injunction to prevent the telecast of a film on the basis that it was likely to be offensive to public feelings. The applicant was accorded standing on the ground that he had sufficient interest as he owned a TV set and had paid his license fee. Lord Denning held the following:

> *"In the light of all this, I believe that, in the last resort, if the Attorney General refuses to leave in a proper case, or improperly or unreasonably delays in giving leave or his machinery works too slowly, then a member of the public, who has a sufficient interest, can himself apply to the Court itself."*

RULE RELAXATION IN PUBLIC INTEREST LITIGATION

In adversarial litigation, the requirement of a party's *locus standi* is compulsory. The legal capacity of the parties (for event, public or private) should be assessed solely based on their competence to respond concerning any requested remedy.[325]

---

322 1961 AC 617

323 (1972) 2 QB 299: (1972) 2 All ER 589.

324 1973 QB 629: (1973) 2 WLR 344: (1973) 1 All ER 689"

325 Janta Dal v. H.S. Chaudhary (1992) 4 SCC 305: 1993 Cr LJ 600: (1992) 4 SCR 226".

In the case of PIL, the *locus standi* law was relaxed. Nevertheless, the relaxation of the rule, however, does not give anybody the right to approach the Court under the guise of a PIL. The court for its own sake, shall not allow its mechanism to be violated by entertaining matters motivated by private profit, policy motive, or some other ambiguous considerations.[326]

To comprehend the *locus standi* concept as well as its relaxation in the PIL case, it is required that the meaning of PIL is clearly understood.

PIL (Public Interest Litigation) involves/encompasses:

– legal actions introduced in a court of law.

– for the enforcement of general interest or public interest.

– wherein the class of community or the public.

– have pecuniary or some interest by which their legal liabilities or rights are affected.[327]

There exist three categories in which applicant can be categorized:

– meddlesome interloper or busybody.

– stranger.

– person aggrieved.

The busybody's application must not be accepted because they do not have any *locus standi* to file a PIL.

Public interest law is a unique American development. There exist several ways to define it. A committee with higher powers, known as *'Juridicare committee'* established by the Indian Government on 19 May 1976 comprising of Supreme Court's two very well-known Judges, Justice V.R. Krishna Iyer and Justice P.N. Bhagwati, observed that in a system that has acquired injustice and inherits it at the very grassroots, there are victims in large numbers. It is extremely difficult for the lower-income groups and the poor to fight for their rights in our expensive court system. Instances where people of a village may be prevented from

326 S.P. Gupta v. Union of India (1991) 3 SCC 161".
327 *Supra* note 389

walking alone a public pathway by a feudal chief, Harijan workers may be denied fair wages, women workers as a class may be refused equal wages are grave concerns that call for class action. Here, representative suits can be entertained when one man's wrong shares a common and similar interest as others. Each one being driven to Court on his separate cause of action is itself a public wrong. The rule of *locus standi* requires being broad-based and any organization (or individual) must be able to start such legal action. And such community proceedings like public interest litigation, class action and the like before Courts, tribunals and other authorities must be financially promoted by legal aid organisations and public interest lawyers.[328]

It has been indicated in *Janta Dal v. H.S. Chowdhury,*[329] that while describing the *locus standi* rule, no rigid litmus test can be applied since the law is under development:

"Though we have, in our country, recognized a departure against the strict rule of locus standi as applicable to a person in private action and broadened and liberalized the rule of standing and thereby permitted a member of the public, having no personal gain or oblique motive to approach the Court for enforcement of the Constitutional or legal rights of socially or economically disadvantaged persons who on account of their poverty or total ignorance of their fundamental rights are unable to enter the portals of the Courts for judicial redress, yet no precise and inflexible working definition has been evolved in respect of locus standi of an individual seeking judicial remedy and various activities in the field of PIL. Probably, some reservation and diversity of approach to the philosophy of PIL among some of the Judges of this Court as reflected against the various decisions of this Court is one of the reasons for this Court finding it difficult to evolve a consistent jurisprudence in the field of PIL".

"True, in defining the rule of locus standi, no 'rigid litmus test' can be applied since the broad contours of PIL are still in developing space, seemingly with a divergent view of several aspects of the concept of this newly developed law and discovered jurisdiction leading to a rapid transformation of judicial

328 *Report on National Juridicare: Equal Justice – Social Justice* Government of India, Ministry of Law, Justice and Company Affairs, p. 61 (1977).

329 AIR 1993 SC 892: (1992) 4 SCC 305.

activism, with a far-reaching change both in the nature and form of the judicial process".

DEFINITIONS OF PIL

The definition of public interest as given in Stroud's Judicial Dictionary[330]:

"Public Interest: A matter of public or general interest does not mean that which is interesting as a gratifying curiosity or a love of information or amusement; but that in which a class of the community have a pecuniary interest or some interest by which their legal rights or liabilities are affected."

In the US, the *Council Public Interest Law* set up by the Ford Foundation in its report,[331] has opted for an extensive definition:

"Public Interest Law is the name that has recently been given to efforts to provide legal representation to previously unrepresented groups and interests. Such attempts have been undertaken in recognition of the fact that the ordinary marketplace for legal services fails to provide such services to significant segments of the population and to significant interest. Such groups and interests include the poor, environmentalists, consumers, racial and ethnic minorities, and others."

Public interest law is described by Rajeev Dhawan as:

"Public Interest Law is part of the struggle by, and on behalf of, the disadvantaged to use 'Law' to solve social and economic problems arising out of differential and unequal distribution of opportunities and entitlements in society.

To procure 'justice between generations', it is also concerned with preventing the present and future needless exploitation of human, natural and technological resources."[332]

330 John S. James, Stroud's Judicial Dictionary, IV (Sweet & Maxwell, 4th edn., 1971-1974).

331 Balancing the Scales of Justice – Financing Public Interest law in America, A Report by the Council Public Interest Law 6-7 (1976).

332 Rao, *supra* note 176

The term "public interest" has not been specified either in the Indian Constitution or in any legislation. However, it is applied under matters affecting the Constitution or the Legislation for example

1.Constitution's Article 302 states that:

"Parliament may by law impose such restrictions on the freedom of trade, commerce or intercourse between one State and another or within any part of the territory of India as may be required in the public interest".

2.Indian Evidence Act's Section 124 states 'Public Interest' as-

"No public officer shall be compelled to disclose communications made to him in official confidence when he considers that the public interests would suffer by the disclosure".

3.Companies Act's Section 396 provided for

Companies' amalgamation in the public interest. Also, for defining public interest, no attempt has been made in this context in the situation.

4.Companies Act's Section 397 states 'Public Interest' as –

Any member of a company who complains that the affairs of the company are being conducted in a manner prejudicial to the public interest or in a manner oppressive to any member or members (including any one or more of themselves) may apply to the Tribunal for an order under this section, provided such members have a right so to apply in virtue of section 399.

INDIAN PERSPECTIVE

Krishna Iyer, J.. initially seeded the idea of PIL in India in *Mumbai Kamgar Sabha v. Abdul bhai*[333] in 1976 (without vocabulary assignment). He had while disposing of an industrial dispute regarding payment of bonus stated that:

"Our adjectival branch of jurisprudence, by and large, deals not with sophisticated litigants but the rural poor, the urban lay and the weaker societal segments for which the law will be an added terror if technical misdescriptions and deficiencies in drafting pleadings and setting out the

333 AIR 1976 SC 1455: (1976) 3 SCC 832.

cause-title create a secret weapon to non-suit a part. Where foul play is absent, and fairness is not faulted, the latitude is a grace of processual justice. Test litigations, representative actions, pro bono public, and like broadened forms of legal proceedings are in keeping with the current accent on justice to the common man and a necessary disincentive to those who wish to bypass the real issues on the merits by suspect reliance on peripheral procedural shortcomings. Even Article 226, viewed on a wider perspective, may be amenable to the ventilation of collective or common grievances, as distinguished from an assertion of individual rights, although the traditional view, backed by precedents has opted for the narrower alternative. Public interest is promoted by a spacious construction of locus standi in our socioeconomic circumstances and conceptual latitudinarianism permits taking liberties with individualization of the right to invoke the higher Court where the remedy is shared by a considerable number, particularly when they are weaker. Less litigation, consistent with a fair process, is the aim of adjective law".

The term *Public Interest Litigation* was utilized in *Fertilizer Corporation Kamgar Union v. Union of India*[334]. In that judgment, Krishna Iyer J used the phrase "epistolary" jurisdictions while delivering his opinion for Bhagwati J and himself.

This rule is gaining momentum day by day, burgeoned further, expanding its branches into the cosmos of PIL, taking its roots firmly in the Indian Judiciary and fully blossomed with fragrant smell as can be read in *S.P. Gupta v. Union of India.*[335]

In *Bar Council of Maharashtra v. M.V. Dabholkar*[336], it has been reported that the Bar Council plays a major role: firstly, to accept complaints; secondly, to develop a rational belief in the consciousness of a professional or awareness of other wrongdoings, and lastly, to refer the matter to its disciplinary committee. The Bar Council has an important role to play. The hearing is conducted by the State Bar Council before the disciplinary committee.

334 "(1981) 2 SCR 52: AIR 1981 SC 344".
335 AIR 1982 SC 149".
336 (1975) 2 SCC 702: AIR 1975 SC 2092".

It is most significant because no litigant and no member of the public can straightaway commence disciplinary proceedings against an advocate. For these purposes, the Bar Council is 'an aggravated person.'[337]

Firstly, the phrase 'person aggrieved' in the Act is of wide import in the context of the purpose and provisions of the statute. In disciplinary proceedings before the disciplinary committee, there is no *lis* and there are no parties. The term 'person' therefore includes the Bar Council which represents the State Bar.

Secondly, the Bar Council is 'an aggravated person' since it represents the collective conscience of the standards of professional conduct and etiquette. The Bar Council functions as the defender of the pureness and integrity of the profession.

Thirdly, the function of the Bar Council in entertaining complaints against advocates is when the Bar Council has a reasonable belief that there is a *prima facie* case of misconduct and that a disciplinary committee is entrusted with such inquiry. Once an inquiry begins, the Bar Council has no control over its decision.

FEATURES OF PIL IN INDIA

In India, the PIL evolution has the following notable salient characteristics:

1. Upholds the supremacy of a written Constitution.
2. A provision that emphasizes a welfare State.
3. Strengthens the provisions of Part IV of the Constitution.
4. Fundamental freedom and Constitutional guarantees' congruence and unique fusion as well as Constitutional obligations that provides a balance of conflicting interests.
5. The fundamental right to move the Supreme Court.
6. The powers of judicial review conferred on the High Court as well as the Supreme Court.

---

337 "(1975) 2 SCC 702: AIR 1975 SC 2092".

A PIL in true sense is one in which a selfless citizen having no personal gain of any kind, except either compassion for the weaker and disabled or deep concern for stopping serious public injury, approaches the court for any of the following purposes:

1. *"Enforcement of fundamental rights of those who genuinely do not have adequate means of access to the judicial system or statutory provisions incorporating the directive principles of State Policy for the amelioration of their condition; and*
2. *Preventing or annulling executive acts and omissions violative of the Constitution or law resulting in substantial injury to the public interest."*[338]

The Supreme Court referred to three phases of the origin and development of PIL in India in the case of *State of Uttaranchal v. Balwant Singh Chaufal*[339]:

Phase I deals with the Supreme Court cases in which directions and orders were mainly passed for the protection of fundamental rights under Article 21 of the Constitution, concerning oppressed communities and sections of society who are unable to approach the Supreme Court or the High Court due to extreme poverty, ignorance, and illiteracy.

Phase II includes the cases related to the preservation and protection of ecology, forests, environment, wildlife, marine life, rivers, mountains, historical monuments, and more.

Phase III addresses the Courts' direction to maintain integrity in governance, transparency, and truthfulness.

GUIDELINES FOR PIL LAID DOWN BY THE APEX COURT

The guidelines have been laid down to preserve the purity and sanctity of the PIL[340]:

338 D. K. Parihar v. Union of India, AIR 2005 Raj 171.

339 AIR 2010 SC 2550 para 45; 2010 AIR SCW 1029: (2010) 3 SCC 402.

340 State of Uttaranchal v. Balwant Singh Chanfal, AR 2010 SC 2550: (2010) 3 SCC 402 (para 181).

i. The Courts must encourage genuine and bona fide PIL and effectively discourage and crush the PIL filed for extraneous considerations.

ii. Instead of every individual Judge devising his procedure for dealing with the PIL, it would be appropriate for each High Court to properly formulate rules for encouraging and discouraging the PIL filed with oblique motives. Consequently, the Supreme Court requests the High Courts which have not framed the rules, should frame the rules within three months. The Registrar General of each High Court is directed to ensure that a copy of the Rules prepared by the High Court is sent to the Secretary-General of the Supreme Court immediately thereafter.

iii. The Court should prima facie verify the credentials of the petitions before entertaining a PIL.

iv. The Court should be prima facie satisfied regarding the correctness of the contents of the petition before entertaining a PIL.

v. The Courts should be fully satisfied that substantial public interest is involved before entertaining the petition.

vi. The Courts should establish that the petition which involves larger public interest, gravity, and urgency must be given priority over other petitions.

vii. The Courts before entertaining the PIL should ensure the PIL is aimed at redressal of genuine public harm or public injury. The courts should also ensure that there is no personal gain, private motive, or oblique motive behind filing the PIL.

viii. The Courts should further ensure that the petitions filed by busybodies for extraneous and ulterior motives must be discouraged by imposing exemplary costs or by adopting similar novel methods to curb frivolous petitions and the petitions filed for extraneous considerations.

In *P. v. Paddington Valuation Officer Ex. P. Peachey Property Corporation Limited*[341]:the court held that:

"Every citizen has the standing to invite the Court to prevent some abuse of power and in doing so, he may claim to be regarded not as a meddlesome busybody but as a public benefactor. A rate-prayer, likewise, has a particular grievance if the rating list is invalidly made, even though the defects will make no difference to him financially".

In the landmark cases of *S.P. Gupta v. Union of India*, *People's Union for Democratic Rights v. Union of India*, and *Bandhua Mukti Morcha v. Union of India*, the Supreme Court evolved a new rule viz., any member of the public acting bona fide and having sufficient interest can maintain an action for redressal of public wrong or public injury.

Voluntary agencies, groups, individuals' charitable organizations, etc. may take such action. The members of the public should not, however, be simply a busy individual or an interloper but a citizen with an adequate interest in the situation. The Supreme Court has laid down:

"Ordinarily only a person whose rights are violated can move a court for redress. However, where there is a likelihood of any Government action injuring the interests of many persons, anyone may move the court for relief."[342]

THE DIFFERENT PHASES OF PIL

The evolution of PIL in India can be viewed under three distinct phases.

First, phase primarily concentrated on the plight of the downtrodden, specifically prisoners. Also, it has been rightly commented by Rajeev Dhavan that:

341 (1966) 1 QB 380(400

342 Bihar Legal Support Society v. Chief Justice of India, AIR 1987 SC 38: (1986) 4 SCC 767: 1986 (4) Supreme Court 264

"The first phase of Indian PIL concerned with the conditions in which men, women, and children were incarcerated in prison and other places of detention."[343]

While the Court has taken swift measures to advance a more rigorous review of administrative action, it did not result in developing a criminal due process. With greater confidence, the court discussed social justice concerns, including the trafficking of bonded labour, working conditions, and compensation for unorganized workers.

Second, the administration came under the scanner of the court, and it gave several landmark judgments giving a fresh interpretation to several Constitutional provisions to make the government more accountable.

The Supreme Court, in *D.C. Wadhwa v. the State of Bihar*[344], ruled that repromulgation of the ordinance was a fraud of the Constitution. The book *'Repromulgation of Ordinances: a Fraud on the Constitution*[345], written in 1983 by Professor Wadhwa, highlights the misuse of authority to pass ordinances.

Third, environment as well as rule of law formed a large corpus of PILs. The steady growth of principles and doctrines that have enriched environmental jurisprudence owe their existence to PIL cases and the accompanying activist approach of the Judiciary.

THE BIRTH OF ENVIRONMENTAL JURISPRUDENCE THROUGH JUDICIAL ACTIVISM

There are many causes of environmental concerns. Some result directly from negative implications of development activity while others could emerge from a lack of development itself. These problems may be of a global impact (like climate change and global warming) or more localized (failure to enforce environmental safeguards in air, water, or noise pollution projects). The right to the environment is

343 Rajeev Dhavan, Law as Struggle: Public Interest Law In India, 36 JILI 308 (1994).

344 AIR 1987 SC 579: (1987) 1 SCC 378.

345 D. C. Wadhwa, Re-promulgation of Ordinances: A Fraud on the Constitution of India (Gokhale Institute, of Politics and Economics, Pune, 1983).

enshrined in every country's fundamental legal structure. The judiciary has consistently affirmed that.[346]

In the *Oleum gas leak* case[347] (the beginning of third phase of PIL), the doctrine of total responsibility for damage caused by hazardous and inherently dangerous industries was drawn by the Supreme Court.

The court right from the case of *Rural Litigation Kendra*,[348] was propounding principles such as 'sustainable development', the 'polluter pays' principle, and adopting certain other principles from international instruments such as the Stockholm Declaration, Rio Declaration, Kyoto Protocol, Biodiversity Convention, the various United Nations Environmental Programmes, etc.

The Court in the *Narmada Bachao Andolan* case,[349] ensured that development by way of building of dams did not take its toll on the employment, shelter, and the homes of people. It directed the State Governments concerned to rehabilitate the displaced people before going ahead.

The Hon'ble Supreme Court recognized the concept of "polluter pays" that has revolutionized the environment conservation movement by keeping the polluter accountable in the light of the principle of absolute liability for compensation for harm caused by him. This was used in cases involving shrimp farms,[350] tanneries[351], chemical

346 Environmental Jurisprudence in India – Part 1, (https://greencleanguide.com/environmentaljurisprudence-in-india-part-1/) last accessed on 15 December 2021

347 M.C. Mehta v. Union of India, AIR 1987 SC 1086: (1987) 1 SCC 395: 1987 ACJ 386.

348 AIR 1987 SC 2426: JT 1987 (5) 122

349 Narmada Bachao Andolan v. Union of India (1999) 8 SCC 308: AIR 1999 SC 3345: 1999 AIR SCW 3841.

350 Vellore Citizen's Welfare Forum v. Union of India (1996) 5 SCC 647: 1996 AIR SCW 3399: AIR 1996 SC 2715.

351 Indian Council for Enviro-Legal Action v. Union of India (1996) 3 SCC 212: AIR 1996 SC 1446: 1996 AIR SCW 1069

industries in Rajasthan[352], and Andhra Pradesh,[353] each of which was found discharging untreated effluents into water bodies or the soil.

M.C. Mehta filed several petitions, and the environment was accepted as a part of right to life. The Court has given numerous guidelines to avoid pollution in the atmosphere and surrounding through various landmark judgments:

- Polluter's liability to pay for pollution[354]
- The government's duty to spread environmental awareness through movie slides or special lessons must be added to the syllabi of schools and colleges[355]
- Phasing out of polluting vehicles[356]
- Protection and conservation of forests[357]
- Solid waste and urban waste management[358]
- Corrosion of Taj Mahal and other historical monuments[359]
- Pollution by the slaughterhouses in Delhi[360] and
- Pollution in Ganga by Kanpur tanneries[361]

352 Indian Council for Enviro-Legal Action v. Union of India, 1995 (6) SCALE 578

353 Bhavani River-Sakthi Sugars Ltd. (1998) 2 SCC 601: AIR 1998 SC 2059: 1998 AIR SCW 1918.

354 M.C. Mehta v. Union of India (also called Oleum Gas case), AIR 1987 SC 965: (1986) 2 SCC 325.

355 M.C. Mehta v. Union of India, AIR 1992 SC 382: (1992) 1 SCC 358.

356 M.C. Mehta v. Union of India, AIR 1999 SC 291: (1999) 6 SCC 12.

357 T.N. Godavarman Thirumulpad v. Union of India, (1997) 2 SCC 267; 3 SCC 312; 7 SCC 440; (1998) 2 SCC 2 SCC 341: AIR 1998 SC 1153.

358 Almitrah Patel v. Union of India, (1998) 2 SCC 416: AIR 1998 SC 1153.

359 M.C. Mehta v. Union of India, (1997) 2 SCC 353: AIR 1997 SC 734.

360 Buffalo Traders' Welfare Association v. Maneka Gandhi, (1996) 11 SCC 35: 1996 (8) SCALE 665.

361 M.C. Mehta v. Union of India, (1997) 2 SCC 441.

Judicial activism has resulted in two astonishing feats in India:[362]

First, the Supreme Court enunciated in the seventies an unusual province and function for judicial review by declaring that the power of Parliament to amend the Constitution was subject to judicial review: it may not extend to alteration of the essential features of the basic structure of the Constitution. What the 'essential features' were, was left for the justices to enunciate from time to time.

Second, the meteoric rise of the social action litigation (SAL, to be distinguished carefully from Public Interest Litigation: PIL) in India represents a process of formalization and democratization of access to appellate courts, including the Supreme Court of India.

FINDINGS

It can be concluded that PIL is a weapon that needs to be used very cautiously and carefully. The judiciary must take great care to rule out any hideous private malice, vested involvement, and/or publicity-seeking behind the veil of public interest. It must be employed as an efficient tool in the legal armoury to provide social justice to the citizen. The attractive Public Interest Litigation brand should not be used for suspicious products of mischief. It should aim at redressal of genuine public wrong/injury and not publicity oriented or founded on a personal vendetta. As elaborated above, Court must be careful to see that anybody or persons or a member of the public, who approaches the Court is acting *bona fide* and not for personal gain or private motive or vide political motivation.

Public Interest litigations have certainly added to the growth of Judicial activism and vice-versa. The judiciary, wherever it finds that the actions on the part of the Legislature or the Executive are illegal or unconstitutional, may step in through the PILs.

'Judicial activism' manifested in the strategy of PIL has paved the way for the participation of public-spirited and enlightened people in India's development process, displaying the potential of the legal system

362 Upendra Baxi, Post-colonial Legality: A Postscript from India, Verfassung und Recht in Übersee/Law And Politics in Africa, Asia And Latin America, 45:2 (2012) 178-194

to offer justice to the poor and the oppressed. The Supreme Court, by taking up such cases, has attempted to show its emerging role as the guardian of the rights and liberties of victims of repression, cruelty, and torture. The Supreme Court of India in its activist role vis-a-vis PIL has taken a goal-oriented approach in the interest of justice by simplifying the highest technical and anachronistic procedures.

In the hands of the Supreme Court, PIL has taken the multidimensional character in India. The age-old adversarial system has been given a go-by. With the advent of judicial activism, letters, newspaper reports, complaints by public-spirited persons,456 social action groups457 bringing to the notice of the Court regarding violation of fundamental rights were accepted and treated as writ petitions, granting relief of compensation through writ jurisdiction under Article 32 of the Constitution.

The existence and practice of Judicial activism are essential because: if there is judicial in-activism, then the dice will be loaded heavily against the citizen who challenges any state action or inaction of public authorities; there is also the fear that Courts may in the process become mere cheerleaders for the Government, rather than guardians of public interest and individual rights. The real thrust stems from the jurisprudence of public duties and faith that the rule of law is used as a formula for expressing the fact that the laws of the Constitution are not the source but the consequence of the rights of the individuals as defined and expressed by Courts.

यतोधर्मस्ततोजयः॥

"Yato dharmas tato jayah"

"Whence law (dharma), thence victory (jayah)"

CONCLUSION AND SUGGESTIONS

Through the judgments and topics discussed in this book, it was repeatedly observed that the Supreme Court being the supreme judicial organization, has always endeavoured hard to be an epitome of justice, thereby follow its motto *yato dharmas tato jayah*.

Constitutions are created with many inherent compromises, some clear written directions, and most undocumented inferences. It is the judiciary that infuses a living status to the unwritten norms through creative interpretation, following the need of the times. Judicial Activism is what fills the vacuum and helps evolve the law.

Judiciary despite being independent of the other two organs of the state, is accountable to the people of the nation through the Constitution. It is the most venerated organ of the State and has evolved itself to become increasingly impactful as the arbiter of justice, *because* the common man has placed his confidence in it.

The lack of concern and want of responsiveness of the legislature and executive in addressing the pressing problems of the people has compelled the courts to enforce the rights of people through the novel and innovative strategies meeting the need of the times. Even in cases of political instability due to the formation of coalition governments, when the legislature and executive are constrained to fulfil their obligations towards the people, the judiciary is looked up to for redressal of people's grievances against the government.

The courts have taken cognizance in the flair of Judicial Activism, addressing almost every aspect of life in the present times be it the case of bonded labour, unlawful detentions, torture and mistreatment of women, implementation of various provisions of the Constitution, environmental issues, health, sports, scam cases, etc. to protect the basic human rights of every member of society.

Justice A.M. Ahmadi, the former Supreme Court Judge, described the activism's current phase in February 1996, in his Zakir Hussain memorial lecture, in the following words:

"Courts would never have resorted to (activism) had the other two democratic institutions functioned effectively."[363]

Governance, however, cannot be substituted by judicial institutions. There is a greater need to discover a balance between Judicial and Executive Institutions. We need to emphasize the balance between reforms, development, and institutions. A balance between the powers of the Judiciary, the Legislature, and the Executive is a must to carry the nation on the true path of democracy. Countries like China, Brazil, and Mexico, with a stronger executive authority, have exhibited better growth dimensions.

'Judicial Activism' should not be used to cause the Constitutional doctrine of separation of power to get eroded. The Hon'ble Judges should not breach their limits in the name of Judicial Activism and take over the functions of other organs of administration.

Judicial pronouncements must respect the demarcations that separate the Legislature, the Executive, and the Judiciary.

Although the politicians and some Constitutional experts criticize judicial activism, the lawyers and the public have appreciated it wholeheartedly. Judicial Activism has many merits, but it has certain demerits too.

The important question today is not whether the Supreme Court could exercise its judicial role, but to what extent the concepts of Judicial Activism and creativity are applied.

Judicial activism has indeed played a vital role in restoring the dignity of the courts during difficult times when the executive has failed the distressed citizen. When the credibility of the judicial institutions is at stake, it the by their actions that the confidence of people can be restored. The judiciary should ensure compliance with the legislative mandate and thereby protect the rights of the citizens.

It is the time when we must bring back those old glories by strengthening the coordination and harmonization between the stakeholders of the Justice Delivery System with the help of harnessing

363 Report, Judiciary Takes Over, Outlook, March 6, 1996, 13.

our extraordinary ability by adopting and practicing the attributes possessed in our legal and political heritage.

In the enlightening words of Karl Marx:

"The Philosophers have only interpreted the world in various ways; The point, however, is to change it."

SUGGESTIONS

This research work elaborates how the higher judiciary, in particular, Supreme Court has, on the whole, played its constitutional role very well and has always upheld the dogma of constitutionalism. In recent years, it has been in the forefront of rendering Justice – Social, Political, and economic, at par with the other two limbs of the government. Judicial activism has played a significant role in Indian democracy. However, because of the danger that could be posed by the judicial activism, and to maintain equilibrium among the three organs of the State, the following suggestions are submitted:

1. There should be a thorough introspection by all the organs of the state so that they can function harmoniously to strengthen the democratic setup.
2. One organ should not try to assert superiority over the other organs of the government. Each organ of the state should understand and respect the constitutional function of the other organs.
3. Judiciary should acknowledge the exasperation of people suffering from a delay in the dispensation of justice and improve its functioning by expediting the process of administration of justice.
4. There is a need to develop healthy conventions amongst the three state organs viz Judiciary, Legislature, and Executive based on mutual respect, as they serve a common purpose by exercising their respective powers. The judiciary should ensure compliance with the legislative mandate and thereby protect the rights of the citizens.

5. Judges must restrain the temptation of publicity, and rid themselves of the belief that the judiciary alone can solve all problems that afflict our society. 'PIL is not a pill for every ill'.
6. Necessary care should be taken to ensure that judicial activism does not become *'judicial adventurism'*, else people would not know which organ of the state to approach, for what problem.
7. The constitutional courts must recognize and remember that 'policy is for the government' and 'law for the court'.
8. Judicial activism should also be applied in cleaning the judiciary itself. The apex court should take prompt action in cases of bribing and corruption against judges. Strict scrutiny of the character and the work done by an advocate should be performed while appointing a person as a judge.
9. The office of the Chief Justice of India and other judges of higher judiciary must be brought under the purview of the Right To Information Act, 2005 as has been decided by the Delhi High Court in *Secretary-General, Supreme Court of India Vs. Subhash Chandra Agarwal*[364] and they should declare their assets and means thereof, before taking the oath of office.
10. The Higher Judiciary must always remember what Mr. Justice Jackson of the United States Supreme Court has said– *'We are not final because we are infallible, but we are infallible because we are final"*. It must further be kept in mind that Constitutional democracy implies interactive understanding of the people, their representatives, and the judiciary together. Therefore, judicial pronouncements and power must be allowed to be scrutinized by people as the actions of the political branches are subject to people's scrutiny. In furtherance of this, there must be some institution not amendable to contempt, draw attention towards apparently wrong judgments, and its findings must be recognized and looked into by the judiciary.

364 AIR 2010 Delhi 159 (Del)

This would result in a lot of improvement in the functioning of the judiciary.

11. The judiciary should always acknowledge the supremacy of the Constitution and not the supremacy of the judiciary. The very reason behind it is that the judiciary has invariably to rely upon the other institutions for the implementation of their orders and directions.

12. The judiciary should be active for noble causes but never at the cost of downgrading other organs of the state, as has been seen in the matter of appointment and transfer of judges and some cases of over activism.

13. Instead of vesting the power to recommend the appointment and transfer of judges of the Higher Judiciary in a collegium of four senior-most judges of the apex court including Chief Justice of India, it would be better to entrust the said power at the hands of a commission comprising judges, representatives of parliament and the central executive, jurists and senior advocates. The recommendatory body would be way more democratic and the appointment of the judges in the higher judiciary would be much more transparent.

14. There must be greater judicial accountability of the judges while ensuring that the legislature and the executive are accountable to the Constitution. There is a need to fix the accountability of individuals and institutions. The judges ought not to forget that they are also equally accountable to the Constitution and ultimately to the people. In this regards ***Judges Accountability Bill, 2010*** which is on the anvil of the parliament is a commendable step.

15. The courts must exercise self-restraint in certain predefined areas where the legislature and the executive have an exclusive role to play.

16. In formulating the directive to the executive, the judiciary should not take it upon itself to decide what fell within the province of the executive. It would be wise to issue a mandate

to the executive in the first instance to perform its duty within a given time frame, failing which it may issue the required writ.

17. The Legislature and Executive being of a representative character must ensure responsible behavior. Judiciary has been the arbiter of the democratic values in India. It must also be mindful of Judicial intolerance, aggressive political posturing and grand standing.

18. The legislature and the executive must share the blame for having conceded space by failing to take timely remedial measures to undo judicial over-reach if any.

19. Judiciary must take care to ensure that its orders are capable of execution, for no amount of judicial activism is useful if its orders are not capable of execution. They should not merely remain ***'paper tigers'***. The feasibility aspects of the orders must be kept in mind while issuing them.

20. Where the matter under complaint involves public policy: the courts should decline to exercise jurisdiction, since the determination of public policy falls outside the domain of matters of judicial review. No writs of certiorari, mandamus, or prohibition should be issued in such cases.

21. Indian Judiciary must be open to accepting challenges as it did during the 'Global Coronavirus Pandemic' and converted the adversities into opportunities for protection of basic human rights as well as our fundamental rights guaranteed by the Constitution of India. The judiciary throughout the nation carried on the process of justice delivery uninterrupted, while strictly adhering to the Special Operation Procedures (SOPs) and the guidelines issued by the Government of India.

22. The Apex court, all High Courts, and the subordinate courts during the coronavirus pandemic period acted as a benevolent crusader for vulnerable sections of the society and that indeed was a novel form of 'judicial activism'.

23. The Supreme Court and the High Courts with the active cooperation of bar members must put in place necessary guidelines to encourage the use of electronic mode for filing (e-filing) of fresh cases and use of video conferencing mode for arguing the e-filed cases which would indeed serve the new and vibrant form of judicial activism visible in recent times.

24. The domain of judicial activism encompasses *inter alia* representative public interest litigations and curative petitions which found their space with ever-increasing dimensions of constitutional laws. Remedies such as the filing of curative petitions were created to serve justice and to negate the existence of any inadvertent error in the dispensation of justice.

25. Similarly, to do something different under the concept of judicial activism, international standards of functioning in the field of the judiciary must be introduced in India and the existing judicial system should be modified accordingly. The introduction of e-courts up to the district level could be a beginning in the direction of the use of technology in our participative judicial system.

26. Functioning of e-courts, e-filing, and digitalization of court- records at different High Courts have begun in the last few years that need to be further extended to the level of subordinate courts. If the concept of judicial activism is to be understood in the modern context, the Courts in addition to the existing dimensions will have to address the ills of the long pendency of civil and criminal cases in Indian Courts and create a mechanism to gradually dissolve the huge backlog of pending cases. It is needless to say that the use of modern-day technology could be of great assistance in reducing the backlog of cases and giving judicial activism a modern outlook.

LIST OF ABBREVIATIONS

All. ER	All England Law Reporters
AIR	All India Reporter
AD	Apex decision
AC	Appeal Cases
Art	Article
Bom. LR	Bombay Law Reporter
Cal.	Calcutta
Cal. LB	California Law Review
CAG	Comptroller and Auditor General
CAT	Central Administrative Tribunal
CBI	Central Bureau of Investigation
CILQ	Central India Law Quarterly
Ch. D	Chancery Division
CJ	Chief Justice
C.P.C	Civil Procedure Code
C.P.C.B	Central Pollution Control Board
Co. Rep.	Company Report
C.r.P.C	Criminal Procedure Code
CVC	Central Vigilance Committee
C.A.D.	Constituent Assembly Debate
Cri.	Criminal
Cri. LJ	Criminal Law Journal
DULJ	Delhi University Law Journals
DB	Division Bench
Edn.	Edition
EIA	Environmental Impact Assessment
FB	Full Bench

GATT	The General Agreement On Tariffs and Trade
Gau.	Gauhati
Harvg. LR	Harvard Law Review
HC	High Court
HP	Himachal Pradesh
Ibid	Ibidem (in the same place)
I.C.J	International Court of Justice
I.P.C	Indian Penal Code
JILI	Journal of the Indian Law Institute
J	Judge
KLT	Kerala Law Times
KB	Kings Bench Division
L.Ed.	Lawyer's Edition, US Supreme Court Reports
LJ	Law Journal
Vis	Namely
N.A.L.S.A	National Legal Services Authority
NGO	Non Government Organization
NOC	Notes On Cases
Ori.	Orissa
Pp	Pages
Pat.	Patna
PC	Privy Council
P.I.L	Public Interest Litigation
Prof.	Professor
P & H	Punjab and Haryana
Punj. LR	Punjab Law Reporter
QB	Queen Bench
QBD	Queen Bench Division
Raj. LW	Rajasthan Law Weekly
SAL	Social Action Litigation
Stan. LR, St.	Stanford Law Review

Supp.	Supplementary
SCC	Supreme Court Cases
SCJ	Supreme Court Journal
SCR	Supreme Court Reporter
SC	Supreme Court
SCW	Supreme Court Weekly
i.e.	That is to say
UDHR	Universal Declaration of Human Rights
UNO	United Nation Organization
U.O.I	Union of India
USA	United States of America
US	United States
V.	Versus
Vol.	Volume
W.T.O	World Trade Organization

LIST OF CASES

- A Parent of a Student of Medical College, Shimla V.State of HP, (1958) 3 SCC169
- A.D.M. Jabalpur V. Shiv Kant Shukla AIR 1976 SC 1207
- A.K. Gopalan V. State of Madras AIR 1950 SC 27: 1950 SCR 88
- A.R.Antulay V.Ramdas Sriniwas Nayak, (1984) 2 SCC 500: AIR 1984 SC 718
- ADM, Jabalpur V. Shivakant Shukla (Habeas Corpus Case) (1976) 2 SCC 521: AIR 1976 SC 1207
- Ajay Hasia V. Khalid Mujib Sehravardi (1981) 1 SCC 722: AIR 1981 SC
- All India Judges Association V. Union of India, (1992) 2 SCC 428
- All India Judges Association V. Union of India, (1998) 2 SCC 204
- Almitra Patel V. Union of India, (1998) 2 SCC 416: AIR 1998 SC 1153
- Ambika Prasad Mishra V. State of UP, (1980) 3 SCC 719: AIR 1980 SC 1762
- Ameerunissa Begum V. Mahboob Begum, 1953 SCR 404: AIR (1953) SC 91
- Anisminic Ltd. V. Foreign Compensation Commission (1962) 2 AC 147; (1969) 1 All. E.R 208
- Apparel Export Promotion Council V. A.K. Chopra (1999) 1 SCC 759

- Aravali Golf Course V. Chander Haas, Appeal (civil) 5732 of 2007
- Aruna Ramchandra Shanbaug V. Union of India, (2011) 4SCC 454
- Ashok Kumar V. Union of India (2008) 6 SCC 1
- Ashwin Kumar Chopra V. Union of India AIR 2011 Del 154
- Asif Hameed V. State of Jammu & Kashmir, AIR 1989 SC 1899
- Assistant Director, Directorate of Enforcement V. Hasan Ali Khan, Appeal (Crl) No 22455/2011
- Attorney General Ex rel. Mcwhirter V. Independent Broadcasting Authority, 1973 QB 629: (1973) 2 WLR 344: (1973) 1 AII ER 689
- Attorney General of Gambia V. N'Jie, 1961 AC 617
- B. Singh V. Union of India, (2004) 3 SCC 363: 367
- Babu Ram Verma V. State of Uttar Pradesh, (1971) AII LJ 653; (1971) Serv LR 649 (1971) 2 Lab LJ 235: (1979) Lab C 1162 (AII
- BALCO Employees Union V. Union of India, (2002).2 SCC 333: AIR 2002 SC 35
- Balco V. Union of India (2002) 2 SCC 333
- Bandhua Mukti Morcha V. Union of India 1984 1 SCC 161, 234
- Bandhua Mukti Morcha V. Union of India, (1984) 3 SCC 161: AIR 1984 SC 802: (1984) 2 SCR 67
- Bandhua Mukti Morcha V. Union of India, AIR 1984 SC 802: (1984) 3 SSC 161: 1984 Lab C 560

- Bar Council of Maharashtra V.M.V. Dabholkar, (1975) 2 SCC 702:AIR 1975 SC 2092
- Basheshar Nath V. Commissioner, Income Tax, AIR 2018 SC 357
- Bhim Singh V. Union of India, (2010) 5 SCC 538
- Bhuwneshwar Singh V. Union of India, (1993) 4 SCC 327
- Bihar Legal Support Society V. Chief Justice of India, AIR 1987 SC 38: (1986) 4 SCC 767: 1986 (4)
- Binny Ltd V. V. Sadasivan, AIR 2005 SC 3202: 2005 AIR SCW 3774: (2005) 6 SCC 657
- Buffalo Traders' Welfare Association V. Maneka Gandhi, (1996) 11 SCC 35: (8) SCALE 665
- Calcutta Gas Co. Ltd. V. State of Bengal, 1962 Supp (3) SCR 1: AIR 1962 SC 1044: 1963 (1) SCJ 106
- CBI V. R.S. Pai, (2002) 5 SCC 82: AIR 2002 SC 1644
- Center Public Interest Litigation & Others V. Union of India & Others, (2011) 1 SCC 560: 2010 (13) SCALE 501:2010 INDLAW SC 1086
- Center of PIL & Anr V. Union of India & Anr (2011) 4 SSC 1
- Charan Lal Sahu V. Giani Zail Singh, (1984) 1 SCC 390: AIR 1984 SC 309: 1984 UJ (SC) 873
- Common Cause V. Union of India, (1996) 6 SCC 593
- Convay V. Rimmer (1967) 1 W.L.R 1031
- D.C Wadhwa V. State of Bihar, AIR 1987 SC 579: (1987) 1 SCC 378

- D.K Basu V. State of W.B (1993) 2 SCC 746
- D.K Basu V. State of West Bengal, (1997) 1SCC 416: 1997 SCC (Cri) 92 : AIR1997 SC610
- D.K Parihar V. Union of India, AIR 2005 Raj
- D.K. Basu V. State of W.B, (1997) 1 SCC 416
- Dalip Singh & Others V. State of Haryana,1993 AIR 1993 SC 2302, 1993 CriLJ 2092, JT 1993 (3) SC 682, 1993 (2) SCALE 671, 1993 Supp (3) SCC 336
- Delhi Judicial Service Asscon V. State of Gujarat AIR 1991 SC 2176
- Divisional Manager, Aravali Golf Club V. Chander Hass, (2007) 14 SCALE 1: (2008) 1 SCC 683: (2008) 1 SCC (L&S) 289
- Dred Scott V. Stanford 60 U.S 393 (1856)
- Emperor V. Sibnath Banerjee, (1946) 48 BOMLR
- Empress V. Burah and Book Singh, (1878) ILR 3 Cal 64
- Fertilizer Corporation Kamgar Union V. Union of India, (1981) 2 SCR 52:AIR 1981 SC 344
- Golaknath V. State of Punjab, AIR 1967 SC 1643
- GridcoiLtd V. Sadananda Doloi, AIR 2012 SC 729
- Hussainara Khatoon V. State of Bihar, AIR 1979 SC 1360:Cr LJ 1036:(1980) 1 SCC 81
- I.C Golak Nath V. State of Punjab, AIR 1967 SC 1643 (1664): 1967 All LJ 813: 1967(2) SCJ 486

- Indian Council for Enviro-Legal Action V. Union of India (1996) 3 SCC 212: AIR 1996 SC 1446: 1996 AIR SCW 1069
- Indian Council for Enviro-Legal Action V. Union of India, 1995 (6) SCALE 578 177
- Indira Gandhi V. Raj Narain AIR 1975 SC 1590
- Indira Nehru Gandhi V. Raj Narain, AIR 1975 SC 2299
- Jagdambika Pal V. Union of India, (1999) 9 SCC 95:AIR 1998 SC 998: 1998 AIR SCW 767
- Janta Dal V. H. S. Chawdhary, AIR 1993 SC 892, 1993 CriLJ 600, 1992 (3) Crimes 199 SC, JT 1992 (5) SC 213, 1992 (2) SCALE 338, (1992) 4 SCC 305, 1992 Supp 1 SCR 226
- Janta Dal V. H.S. Chowdhury, 1993 AIR SCW 248
- Jasbhai Motibhai Desai V. Roshan Kumar, (1976) 1 SCC 671
- K.K.Kochuni V. Madras and Kerala, 1960 AIR 1080.
- Kachchh Jal Sankat Nivaran Samiti V. State of Gujarat AIR 2011 SC 2747: 2011 AIR SCW 4336: (2011) 8 SCALE 26
- Kameshwar Singh V. State of Bihar, (1984) 32 BLJR 522
- Kanaka Rana V. State of Orissa, AIR 2009 Orissa 17
- Kapila Hingorani (1) V. State of Bihar, (2003) 6 SCC 1
- Kaplia Hingorani (2) V. State of Bihar (2005) 2 SCC (L&S) 206
- Kehar Singh & Anr. V. Union of India & Anr., AIR 1989 SC 653: 1989 Cri LJ 941: JT 1988 (4) SC 693: 1988 (2) SCALE 1965: (1989) 1 SCC 204

- Kesavananda Bharati V. State of Kerala, (1973) 4 SSC 225: AIR 1973 SC 1461 100
- Kharak Singh V. State of UP
- Khatri V. State of Bihar (1981) 1 SCC 627
- Kihoto Hollohan V. Zachillhu SCC 651; AIR 1993 SC 412
- Kishor Samrite V. State of Uttar Pradesh, (2013) 2 SCC 398
- Kuldip Nayar V. Union of India (2006) 7 SCC 1: AIR 2006 SC 3127
- L.C Golaknath v. State of Punjab AIR 1967 SC 1643
- I.R Coelho V. State of T.N, (1999) 7 SCC 580
- I.R. Coelho V. State of Tamil Nadu, (2007) 2 SCC1: AIR 2007 SC 861
- Lakshmikant Pandey V. Union of India, (1984) 2 SCC 454
- Liverpool Taxi Owner's Assn, re, (1972) 2 QB 299; (1972) 2 A11 ER 589
- M.C Mehta V. State of Tamil Nadu AIR 1997 SC 699: (1996) 6 SCC 756
- M.C Mehta V. Union of India (also called Oleum Gas), AIR 1987 SC 965 : (1986) 2 SCC 325
- M.C Mehta V. Union of India, AIR 1987 SC 1086: (1987) ACJ 386
- M.C. Mehta V. Union of India, (1987) 1 SCC 395

- M.C. Mehta V. Union of India, (1997) 2 SCC 353: AIR 1997 SC 734
- M.C. Mehta v. Union of India, (1997) 2 SCC 441
- M.C. Mehta V. Union of India, AIR 1992 SC 382: (1992) 1 SCC 358
- M.C. Mehta V. Union of India, AIR 1999 SC 291: (1999) 6 SCC 12
- M.P. Oil Extraction V. K.N Oil Industries (1997) 7 SCC 592: AIR 1998 SC 145P: 1997 AIR SCW 4104
- M.R. Balaji and Others V. State of Mysore, 963 AIR 649, 1962 SCR Supl. (1) 439
- Madhav Rao Scindia V. Union of India, AIR 1970 SC 530
- State of Madras V. Champakam Doriarajan, C.M.Ps Nos. 5255 and 5340 of 1950
- Maneka Gandhi V. Union of India (AIR 1978 SC 597)
- Minerva Mills V. Union of India 1980 AIR 1789 1981 SCR(1) 206 1980 SCC (3)625
- Missouri V. Holland 252 U.S 416, 433 (1920)
- Mohd. Ahmed Khan v. Shan Bano Begum (1985)2 SCC 556
- Mumbai Kamgar Sabha V. Abdulhai, AIR 1976 SC 1455: (1976) 3 SCC 832
- N. Nagendra Rao & Co. V. State of AP, (1994) 6 SCC 205
- Nandani Sundar V. State of Chhattisgarh, Writ petition (Civil) no. 250 of 2007

- Narmada Bachao Andolan V. Union of India (1999) 8 SCC 308: AIR 1999 SC 3345: 1999 AIR SCW 3841
- National Textile Workers Union V. P.R. Ramakrishnan, (1983) 1 SCC 228: AIR 1983 SC75
- Niharendu Dutt Majumdar V. Emperor, AIR 1939 Cal 703.
- Nilabal Bahera alias Lalita Bahera V. Union of Orissa, 1993 AIR 1960 1993 SCR (2) 581 1993 SCC (2) 746 JT 1993 (2) 503
- P. V. Paddingtom Valuation Officer Ex. P. Peachy Property Corporation Limited, (1966) 1 QB 308 (400)
- P.A Namdar V. State of Maharashtra, (2005) 6 SCC 537: AIR 2005 SC 3226
- P.V. Kapoor V. Union of India, 1992 Cri LJ 128 at 137, 138 (Del)
- Padfield V. Minister of Agriculture, Fisheries and Food (1968) AC 997; (1968) 1 All. E.R. 694
- Parmanand Katara V. Union of India, (1989) 4 SCC 286
- People's Union for Democratic Rights V. Union of India, AIR 1982 SC 1473: (1982) 2 SCR 494: (1982) 2 SCWR 202
- Pradeep Kumar Biswas V. India Institute of Chemical Biology (2002) 5 SCC 111:2002 SCC (L&S) 633
- Prakash Singh Badal V. Union of India, AIR 1987 P&H 263
- R. V. Commissioner of Police of Metropolis, ex p Blackburn, (1968) 2 QB 118: (1968) 2 ELR 893: (1968) 1 AII ER 763 (CA)
- R.C. Cooper V. Union of India, AIR 1970 SC 564 ; 1970 SCR (3) 530

- R.E Rustom Cavasjee Cooper V. Union of India, AIR 1970 SC 564
- Raghunathrao Ganapatrao V. Union of India, SCC 191: AIR 1993 SC 1267
- Rajasthan SEB V. Mohan Lal AIR 1967 SC 1857: (1967) 3 SCR 377
- Rajesh Maan V. Delhi Metro Rail Corporation AIR 2010 Del 396 (NOC).
- Rajindera Singh (Dead) Through Lrs. V. Prem Mai & Others, Appeal (civil) 1307 of 2001
- Ram Jawaya Kapur V. State of Punjab, AIR 1955 SC 549
- Ram Jethmalani & Others V. Union of India, Writ Petition (Civil) No(s). 176 of 2009 with SLP (c) no. 11032 of 2009
- Ramakrishna Singh V. State of Mysore, AIR 1960 Kant 338, AIR 1960 Mys 338, ILR 1959 KAR 740
- Ramana Dayaram Shetty V. International Airport Authority of India (1979) 3 SCC 489: AIR 1979 SC 1682
- Rameshwar Prasad & Others (vi) V. Union of India & Anr., (2006) 2 SCC.
- Ranjit Singh V. State of Orissa, AIR 2009 NOC 1047 (Ori)
- Re Bhavani River-Sakthi Sugars Ltd. (1998) 2 SCC 601: AIR 1998 SCC 2059: 1998 AIR SCW 1918
- Ridge V. Baldwin (1964) AC 40
- Romesh Thappar V. State of Madras, (1950) 1 SCR 594, (1950) CRILJ 1514, AIR 1950 SC 124

- Rudal Sah V. State of Bihar (1983) 4 SCC 141
- Rural Litigation Kendra Case, AIR 1987, SC 2426: JT 1987 (5) 122
- S.P Gupta V. Union of India (1981) Supp SCC 87
- S.P Gupta V. Union of India, 1981 Supp SCC 87: AIR 1982 SC 149
- S.P. Gupta V. Union of India (1991) 3 SCC 161
- S.P. Gupta V. Union of India, AIR 1982 SC 149: (1982) 2 SCR 365: 1981 (Supp) SCCC 87
- S.P. Gupta V. Union of India, AIR 1982 SC 149
- S.P. Sampath Kumar V. Union of India (1987) 1 SCC 124:AIR 1987 SC 386
- S.R. Bommai V. Union of India, (1990) 3 SCC 1: AIR 1994 SC 1998
- Sajjan Singh V. State of Rajasthan, 1965 AIR 845 1965 SCR (1) 933
- Sakal Newspapers Private Ltd. V. Union of India, SCR 1960 (2) 671
- Sarla Mudgal V. Union of India (1995) 3 SCC 635: AIR 1995 SC 1531
- Sebastian M. Hongray V. Union of India, 1984 AIR 571 1984 SCR (1) 904 1984 SCC (1) 339 1983 SCALE (2)775 ACT
- Shankari Prasad Singh Deo V. Union of India, 1 SCR 89, AIR 1951 SC 458, 1951 (II) MLJ 683 (SC), 1951 SCJ 775, 1952 SCR 89, (1951) 64 LW 1005

- Shankari Prasad V. Union of India AIR 1951 SC 458
- Sheela Barse V. Union of India, (1988) 4 SCC 226: AIR 1988 SC 2211: JT 1988 (3) SC 765
- Shiv Sagar Tiwari V. Union of India, (1996) 6 SCC 599
- Shri Sachidanand Pandey V. State of West Bengal, AIR 1987 SC 1109
- Smt. Indira Gandhi V. Raj Narain (AIR 1975 SC 2299)
- Som Prakash Rekhi V. Union of India, 1981 AIR 212 1981 SCR (2) 111 1981 SCC (1) 449
- State of Bihar V. Bal Mukund Shah, (2000) 4 SCC 640
- State of Bihar V. Balmukund Shah AIR 2000 SC 1296
- State of Kerala V. Peoples Union Civil Liberties (2009) 8 SCC 46
- State of Punjab V. Rajesh Syal AIR 2002. SC 3687 etc
- State of Rajasthan V. Union of India, (1977) 3 SCC 592, AIR 1977 SC 136
- State of Rajasthan V. Union of India, (1997) 3 SCC 592
- State of U.P. V. Jeet S. Bisht, Appeal (civil) 2740 of 2007
- State of U.P. V. Johri Mal AIR 2004 SC 3800: 2004 AIR SCW 3888: (2004) 4 SCC 714
- State of Uttaranchal V. Balwant Singh Chanfal, AIR 2010 SC 2550 para 45; 2010 AIR SCW 1029: (2010) 3 SCC 402
- State of W.B V. Bela Banerjee, AIR 1954 SC 170

- State of W.B. V. Union of India, AIR 1996 Cal 181, 196: (1996) Com LJ 258
- State of West Bengal & Ors V. Committee for Protection of Democratic Rights, West Bengal & Ors, (2001) 2 CALLT 526 HC, 2001 (2) CHN 98, 2001 CriLJ 2307
- State of West Bengal V. Subodh Gopal, 1954 AIR 92 1954 SCR 587
- State V. Union of India, AIR 1996 Cal 191: (1996) 1 Com LJ 25
- Sunil Batra (2) V. Delhi Admn (1980) 3 SCC 488: AIR 1980 SC 1579
- Supreme Court Advocates-on-Record Assn V. Union of India (1993) 4 SCC 441: AIR 1994 SC 268
- Supreme Court Bar Association V. U.O.I AIR 1998 SC 1895
- Supreme Court Bar Association V. Union of India, (1998) 4 SCC 409, 431- 32
- Supreme Court on Record Association V. Union of India [(1994) 4 SCC 441]
- Swami Shraddhananda @ Murali Manohar Mishra V. State of Karnataka AIR SC 2008 3040: (2008) 11 SCR 93 416
- T.M.A. Pai Foundation V. State of Karnataka (2002) 8 SCC 481: AIR 2003 SC 355
- T.N. Godavaraman Thirumulpad V. Union of India, (1997) 2 SCC 267; 3 SCC 312; 7 SCC 440; (1998) 2 SCC 341: AIR 1998 SC 1153
- Thomas Bonham V. College of Physicians, (1908) 8 Co Rep 113

- Union Carbide Corpn V. U.O.I AIR 1992 SC 248
- Union of India V. Dr. Kushala Shetty, AIR 2011 SC 3210: 2011 AIR SCW 4460: (2011) 7 SCALE 654
- Union of India V. Prakash Singh & Others, JT 2006 (12) SC 225: (9) SCALE 444: (2006) 8 SCC 1
- Union of India V. Sushil Kumar Modi, (1997) 4 SCC 771: (1998) 8 SCC 661
- Union of Indian V. Deoki Nandan Agarwal, 1992 AIR 96 1991 SCR (3) 873 1992 SCC Supl. (1) 323 JT 1991 (3) 608 1991 SCALE (2)481
- Upendra Baxi (1) V. State of U.P., (1983) 2 SCC 308
- Veena Sethi V. State of Bihar, (1982) 2SCC 583: AIR 1983 SC 339
- Vellore Citizens' Welfare Fourm V. Union of India(1996) 5 SCC 647: 1996 AIR SCW 3399: AIR 1996 SC 2715
- Vineet Narain V. Union of India, (1996) 2 SCC 199
- Vineet Narain V. Union of India, (1998) 1 SCC 226, 266
- Vishakha and Others V. State of Rajasthan AIR 1997 SC 3011: JT 1997 (7) SC 45
- Woman Rao V. Union of India, (1981) 2 SCC 362: AIR 1981 SC 271

SOME REMARKABLE JUDGMENTS REGARDING JUDICIAL ACTIVISM

1. *B. Vijayalakshmi v. R. Amaravathi*[365] - decided by Madurai Bench of Madras High Court in July 2020
2. *Babulal and Ors. v. Resmabai Narayanrao Kaurati and Ors.*[366] – decided by Nagpur Bench of Bombay High Court in January 2019
3. *Bharat Jhunjhunwala v. Union of India and Ors.*[367] – decided by Allahabad High Court in January 2019
4. *Kusuma v. State of U.P. and Ors*[368]- decided by Lucknow Bench of Allahabad High Court in January 2019
5. *V. Rama Rao v. Union of India and Ors.*[369] – decided by Madras High Court in January 2019
6. *Satta Panchayat Iyakkam v. State of Tamil Nadu and Ors.*[370] – decided by Madras High Court in February 2019
7. *Sartaj Ahmad Ganie and Ors. v. State and Ors.*[371] – decided by J&K High Court in February 2019
8. *P. Kumaravel v. The District Collector, Collectorate, Salem and Ors.*[372] – decided by Madras High Court in February 2019
9. *G. Vijayakumar v. The Director General, (Personnel), Railway Board and Ors.*[373] – decided by Madras High Court in February 2019

---

365 2020 (3) RCR (Criminal) 775
366 2019 (1) RCR (Civil) 605
367 2019 (1) ADJ 1837
368 2019 (1) ACR 623
369 2019 (3) CTC 306
370 MANU/TN/0742/2019
371 2019 LabIC 1827
372 MANU/TN/1547/2019
373 MANU/TN/2248/2019

10. *Rajiv Kumar v. State of U.P. and Ors.*[374] – decided by Allahabad High Court in March 2019
11. *Tamil Nadu Health Employees Welfare Association v. The Chief Election Commissioner Election Commission of India and Ors.*[375] – decided by Madras High Court in March 2019
12. *S. Hemanathan v. The Director General of Police, Tamil Nadu and Ors.*[376] - decided by Madras High Court in March 2019
13. *Letkhomang Khongsai v.* The State of Manipur and Ors.[377] – decided by Manipur High Court at Imphal in March 2019
14. *Parmar Ramsinh Nathabhai and Ors. v. State of Gujarat and Ors.*[378] – decided by Gujarat High Court at Ahmedabad in April 2019
15. *J. Mohamed Ali v. General Manager, Southern Railway and Ors.*[379] – decided by Madras High Court in April 2019
16. *K. Lakshminarayan v. Union of India and Ors.*[380] – decided by Madras High Court in April 2019
17. *Aarshya Gulati and Ors. v. Government of NCT of Delhi and Ors.*[381] – decided by Delhi High Court in May 2019
18. *E. Murugaesan v. The Registrar General, High Court of Madras and Ors.*[382] – decided by Madras High Court in June 2019
19. *M. Mahendran v. The Director General of Police and Ors.*[383] – decided by Madurai Bench of Madras High Court in July 2019

---

374 2019 (4) ADJ 316
375 MANU/TN/1382/2019
376 MANU/TN/1259/2019
377 2019 (4) GLT 94
378 2019 GLH (2) 40
379 MANU/TN/1857/2019
380 2019 (5) CTC 247
381 2019 (3) RCR (Civil) 236
382 2019 (4) SLR 598
383 MANU/TN/3523/2019

20. *Ruchi Malls Pvt. Ltd. v. State of Gujarat*[384] – decided by Gujarat High Court at Ahmedabad in July 2019
21. *Management of Federal Mogul Goetze India Pvt. v. Additional Labour Commissioner (Administration) and Appellate Authority and Ors.*[385] – decided by Karnataka High Court at Bengaluru in July 2019
22. *P. Velmurugan v. The State of Tamil Nadu and Ors.*[386]– decided by Madurai Bench of Madras High Court in July 2019
23. *M. Senthilkumar v. The Tamil Nadu Uniformed Service and Ors.*[387] – decided by Madurai Bench of Madras High Court in August 2019
24. *M. Mahendran v. The Superintendent of Police, Theni District*[388] – decided by Madurai Bench of Madras High Court in August 2019
25. *V. Swathi v. Principal Secretary to Government, Rural Development and Panchayat Raj Department and Ors.*[389]– decided by Madras High Court in September 2019
26. *Ashwani Kumar v. Union of India (UOI) and Ors*[390]– decided by Supreme Court of India in September 2019
27. *Vijay Namdeorao Wadettiwar and Ors. v. The State of Maharashtra and Ors.*[391]– decided by Bombay High Court in September 2019
28. *Sunit Arora v. MP Public Service Commission and Ors.*[392]– decided by Indore Bench of Madhya Pradesh High Court in September 2019

---

384 MANU/GJ/1292/2019
385 2019 (6) KarLJ 20
386 MANU/TN/4078/2019
387 MANU/TN/4803/2019
388 MANU/TN/4786/2019
389 2020 (2) LLN 760 (Mad.)
390 (2020) 13 SCC 585
391 2019 (6) ABR 205
392 MANU/MP/1287/2019

29. *Amitoj Singh v. Sardar Patel Vidyalaya and Ors.*[393] – decided by Delhi High Court in September 2019
30. *Hassan Thermal Power Plant Pvt. Ltd. v. State of Karnataka and Ors.*[394] – decided by Karnataka High Court at Bengaluru in September 2019
31. *Dist. Collector, Satara and Ors. v. Mangesh Nivrutti Kashid*[395] - decided by Supreme Court of India in October 2019
32. *Court on its own motion v. Union of India and Ors.*[396] – decided by Punjab and Haryana High Court in October 2019
33. *T.K. Abdul Asees v. Medical Council of India and Ors.*[397] – decided by Kerala High Court at Ernakulam in October 2019
34. *Mukhar Hussain T.P. v. Union of India and Ors.* – decided by Kerala High Court at Ernakulam in October 2019
35. *Mythri Residents Association v. Secretary, Tripunitura Municipality and Ors.*[398] – decided by Kerala High Court at Ernakulam in October 2019
36. *Abhishek Pandey v. State of Chhattisgarh and Ors.*[399] – decided by Chhattisgarh High Court at Bilaspur in November 2019
37. *Central Public Information Officer, Supreme Court of India v. Subhash Chandra Agarwal*[400] - decided by Supreme Court of India in November 2019
38. *Amit Singh v. Sandhya Singh*[401] - decided by Lucknow Bench of Allahabad High Court in November 2019

393 MANU/DE/3146/2019
394 2020 (2) ARBLR 142 (Kar)
395 (2019) 10 SCC 166
396 MANU/PH/1486/2019
397 MANU/KE/4457/2019
398 ILR 2019 (4) Kerala 839
399 2020 (1) MPJR (SC) 11
400 (2020) 5 SCC 481
401 (2019) ILR 12 All 1031

39. *K. Raja and Ors. v. The Additional Chief Secretary to Government, Highways and Minor Ports Departments and Ors.*[402] – decided by Madras High Court in November 2019

40. *Shahbaz Ali Khan v. Union of India and Ors.*[403] – decided by Allahabad in December 2019

41. *Ajay Singh v. Union of India and Ors.*[404] – decided by Allahabad High Court in December 2019

42. *Sanket Sahu v. State of M.P. and Ors.*[405] – decided by Gwalior Bench of Madhya Pradesh High Court in December 2019

43. *Rupesh Kumar Singh and Ors. v. The Union of India and Ors.*[406] – decided by Patna High Court in December 2019

44. *Runjhun Solanki v. State of M. P. and Ors.*[407] – decided by Gwalior Bench of Madhya Pradesh High Court in December 2019

45. *Krishna Mahadevan v. K.R. Moniamma and Ors.*[408] – decided by Kerala High Court at Ernakulam in December 2019

46. *Bhagwati v. Cheduram and Ors.*[409] – decided by Chhattisgarh High Court at Bilaspur in December 2019

47. *Shruthi Das Shetty v. Union of India, Ministry of Labour & Employment, Government of India and Ors.*[410] – decided by Central Administrative Tribunal, Bangalore Bench in January 2020

48. *Solomon Thomas v. The State of Kerala and Ors.*[411] – decided by Kerala High Court at Ernakulam in January 2020

---

402 2019 (6) CTC 750
403 (2020) ILR 2 All 317
404 (2020) ILR 2 All 400
405 MANU/MP/2173/2019
406 2020 (1) BLJ 640
407 2020 (3) MPLJ 334
408 2020 (1) KLT 845
409 2020 (2) CGLJ 236
410 MANU/CA/0368/2020
411 MANU/KE/0355/2020

49. *Surjotin and Ors. v. Chamrin Bai and Ors.*[412] – decided by Chhattisgarh High Court at Bilaspur in January 2020
50. *Alok Yadav v. State of M. P. and Ors.*[413] – decided by Indore Bench of Madhya Pradesh High Court in February 2020
51. *Soman K. v. Chief Secretary, State of Kerala, and Ors.*[414] – decided by Kerala High Court at Ernakulam in February 2020
52. *Roopautin Bai v. Sunderi Bai and Ors.*[415] – decided by Chhattisgarh High Court at Bilaspur in February 2020
53. *Maniyar Sai and Ors. v. Jangi Bai and Ors.* – decided by Chhattisgarh High Court at Bilaspur in February 2020
54. *George Vattukulam v. The State of Kerala and Ors.*[416]–decided by Kerala High Court at Ernakulam in February 2020
55. *Gaurav Pandey v. Union of India and Ors.*[417]–decided by Gwalior Bench of Madhya Pradesh High Court in February 2020
56. *G. Hari Govinda Prasad and Ors. v. State of Andhra Pradesh and Ors.*[418] – decided by Andhra Pradesh High Court at Amravati in March 2020
57. *Shafeeq Shahul Hameed v. State of Kerala and Ors.*[419] – decided by Kerala High Court at Ernakulam in May 2020
58. *Arjun Aggarwal v. Union of India and Ors.*[420]–decided by Delhi High Court in June 2020

412 MANU/CG/0066/2020
413 2020 LabIC 2819
414 MANU/KE/0374/2020
415 MANU/CG/0143/2020
416 MANU/KE/0718/2020
417 2020 (4) CGLJ 12
418 2020 (5) ALD 295
419 MANU/KE/1400/2020
420 MANU/DE/1233/2020

59. *B. Vijayalakshmi v. R. Amaravathi*[421]-decided by Madurai Bench of Madras High Court in June 2020
60. *C.M. Subramanian v. District Registrar General, Chembukkavu and Ors.*[422] – decided by Kerala High Court at Ernakulam in June 2020
61. *Joby Sebastian v. The State of Kerala and Ors.*[423] – decided by Kerala High Court at Ernakulam in June 2020
62. *B. Radhakrishna Menon v. State of Kerala and Ors.*[424] – decided by Kerala High Court at Ernakulam in June 2020
63. *Green Vistas Infrastructure Projects v. Union of India and Ors.*[425] – decided by Kerala High Court at Ernakulam in June 2020
64. *Rakesh Kumar Choudhary and Ors. v. Union Territory of J&K and Ors.*[426]–decided by J&K High Court at Jammu in September 2020
65. *Thoufeek Ahamed v. Union of India*[427]–decided by Kerala High Court at Ernakulam in September 2020
66. *M.P. Chothy v. State of Kerala and Ors.*[428]–decided by Kerala High Court at Ernakulam in September 2020
67. *Trinity Infrastructure v. State of M.P. and Ors.*[429]–decided by Jabalpur Bench of Madhya Pradesh High Court in September 2020
68. *Trinity Infrastructure v. State of M.P. and Ors.*[430]–decided by Jabalpur Bench of Madhya Pradesh High Court in September 2020

421 2020 (3) RCR (Criminal) 775
422 MANU/KE/1742/2020
423 MANU/KE/1677/2020
424 MANU/KE/1717/2020
425 MANU/KE/1688/2020
426 MANU/JK/0355/2020
427 MANU/KE/2639/2020
428 MANU/KE/2685/2020
429 2020 (4) MPLJ 511
430 MANU/MP/1376/2020

69. *Ferrodous Estates (Pvt.) Ltd. v. P. Gopirathnam (Dead) and Ors.*[431]– decided by Supreme Court of India in October 2020

70. *Kehar Singh and Ors. v. State of Himachal Pradesh and Ors.*[432]– decided by Himachal Pradesh High Court at Shimla in October 2020

71. *R. Kalyanam v. State of Tamil Nadu and Ors.*[433]–decided by Madras High Court in October 2020

72. Lalitpur Power Generation Company Limited v. Uttar Pradesh Electricity Regulatory Commission and Ors.[434]– decided by Appellate Tribunal for Electricity, New Delhi in November 2020

73. Bendangyanger and Ors. v. State of Nagaland and Ors.[435]– decided by Kohima Bench of Gauhati High Court in November 2020

74. *Labh Singh v. Union of India and Ors.*[436]–decided by Punjab and Haryana High Court in December 2020

75. *Rajeev Suri v. Delhi Development Authority and Ors.*[437]– decided by Supreme Court of India in January 2021

76. *Jhuli and Ors. v. Patru and Ors.*[438]–decided by Chhattisgarh High Court in February 2021

77. *Vora Zakirhusain Valibhai v. State of Gujarat*[439]-decided by Gujarat High Court at Ahmedabad in February 2021

78. *Krishnan M.C. and Ors. v. State of Kerala and Ors.*[440]–decided by Kerala High Court at Ernakulam in February 2021

431 AIR 2020 SC 5041
432 2021 (1) ShimLC 143
433 2020 (2) WritLR 784
434 MANU/ET/0065/2020
435 2020 (5) GLT 486
436 2021 (2) SCT 98 (P&H)
437 MANU/SC/0001/2021
438 MANU/CG/0384/2021
439 MANU/GJ/0214/2021
440 MANU/KE/0350/2021

79. *SV Chiranjivi and Ors. v. The State of Andhra Pradesh*[441]-decided by Andhra Pradesh High Court at Amravati in March 2021

80. *G.V. Seshamamba and Ors. v. State of Andhra Pradesh and Ors.*[442]–decided by Andhra Pradesh High Court at Amravati in March 2021

81. *Agriculture Produce Market Committee v. Mansingh Khadaksing Bhist and Ors.*[443]–decided by Gujarat High Court at Ahmedabad in June 2021

82. *Red Giant Movies v. The Commissioner, Commercial Tax Department, Chepauk and Ors.*[444]–decided by Madras High Court in July 2021

83. *Taj Muhammad and Ors. v. Oil and Gas Development Company Limited and Ors.*[445]–decided by Islamabad High Court in February 2021

84. *Shumaila Salman Shah and Ors. v. Federation of Pakistan and Ors.*[446]–decided by Sukkur Bench of Sindh High Court in May 2021

441 MANU/AP/0306/2021
442 2021 (2) ALT 471
443 MANU/GJ/0763/2021
444 MANU/TN/4645/2021
445 LEX/HIPK/0029/2021
446 LEX/SKPK/0256/2021

Marbury v. Madison[447]

The case *Marbury v. Madison* (1803) saw the U.S. Supreme Court assert for itself and Congress-created lower courts the power of judicial review. A process by which legislation, as well as executive and administrative actions, that were deemed inconsistent with the U.S. Constitution could be declared unconstitutional and therefore null and void. State courts eventually assumed a parallel function with respect to state constitutions.

William Marbury's case arose after the administration of President Thomas Jefferson withheld a judgeship commission that had been formally drafted under the previous president's administration but hadn't been delivered before Jefferson's inauguration.

As per the Supreme Court, the law that would allow it to do so would have been unconstitutional, thus the commission could not be handed over to Marbury.

This case is significant for its establishment of judicial review for the U.S. Supreme Court and lower federal courts with respect to the Constitution, and later for parallel state courts with respect to state constitutions. It would help ensure that the judiciary remains an equal branch of government alongside the legislative and executive branches.

The federal judiciary used judicial review to check the actions of Congress and the president, while remaining a coequal branch of government with them.

447 5 U.S. 137 (1803)